A Chuckle From Heaven:

Bible Stories In-Between The Lines

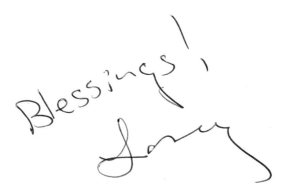

Blessings!

Larry

Written by Larry Beman

Larry Beman
www.chucklefromheaven.com
Larry@ChuckleFromHeaven.com

Library of Congress Control Number: 2010909158
ISBN 978-0-9844971-0-2
Published and printed in Rochester, NY.

This book has been published by process:CREATIVITY Publishing Company, with the guidance of Betta Book Publishing. For more information, please visit www.BettaBookPublishing.com.

Publishing Guide, Editor, Layout: Kelly Sabetta
Author: Larry Beman

process:CREATIVITY
Publishing Company

Table of Contents

1. Introduction.. i
2. Our Story.. 1
3. The Garden (Genesis 3).. 7
4. Abraham (Genesis 12-21)..13
5. Showdown at Mizpah (Genesis 31:43-49)....................15
6. You Want Me to do What? (Exodus 3-4)......................21
7. Parents (Exodus 13:21-22)..25
8. Pillar of Fire (Exodus 13:21)......................................28
9. Gideon (Judges 6-8)...31
10. Singing Woman (1 Samuel 1-2)..................................37
11. Eli (1 Samuel 1-2)..41
12. The First King (1 Samuel 8-31).................................45
13. Michal (1 Samuel 18-19; 25:44. 2 Samuel 3:12-17;
        6:16-23)...49
14. David (1 and 2 Samuel)..53
15. Sarah (The Psalms)...57
16. Be Still (Psalm 46)...61
17. Be Still, and Know (1 Kings 19; Mark 1)...................63
18. Exile (2 Kings)..67
19. Last Thoughts (Esther)..71
20. The Sailor (Jonah)..75
21. Immigration Reform (Ruth).......................................79
22. Heaven and Hell...87

23. A Baby's Crying...91
24. Jacob's Friend (Matthew 1:18-25)..................93
25. What If? (Luke 2:1-20)..................................95
26. Son of God...99
27. Herod (Luke 3:1-14; Mark 6:14-29)...............103
28. The Invitation (Mark 1:16-20).........................107
29. Furious (Luke 4:14-30)....................................111
30. Our Father (Matthew 6:7-15)..........................115
31. Barefoot in a Pig Sty (Luke 15:11-32).............119
32. The Jericho Road (Luke 10:25-37)...................125
33. I See (John 9)..129
34. The Storm (Mark 4:35-41)..............................133
35. Resort Town (Matthew 16:13-23; Mark 8:27-38;
        Luke 9:18-23) 137
36. A Centurion's Report (Mark 11:111)................141
37. It's Over (Mark 14-15)....................................145
38. A Chuckle from Heaven (Luke 24:112).............149
39. Standing at the Door (Acts 12:117)..................151
40. In Jail (Acts 16)..155
41. Dear Paul (Philemon)......................................159
42. All Things New (Revelation 21:5)....................163

Introduction

I was never cut out to be a "preacher." Oh, I tried hard enough. I made every effort to measure up to what I thought someone standing behind a pulpit on Sunday mornings should be. What I got for my efforts was an upset stomach and a feeling of absolute terror every Saturday night. It took a long time to figure out, but the solution was relatively simple. I needed to give up on the idea that I would ever be the preacher of my "shoulds." So I did.

Over time, I came to think of myself as a minstrel, a teller of tales. I found the Bible to be a gold mine of stories waiting to be told through word and song, and I couldn't wait to tell them. The beauty of story-telling was that I didn't need to be the "keeper of the answers," as if I ever was. Stories hold "truth" in their own right; they leave it to the listener to sort out meaning and implication.

"A Chuckle from Heaven" takes a sideways look at the stories found in the Bible and retells them from a variety of points of view. To be sure, I did the necessary digging and research. Then, I let my imagination take control. What was David thinking as he lay on his deathbed? How would a sailor react to being on a ship with Jonah? What would a Roman soldier do if he stood guard on that first Palm Sunday? In the end, I did not find the stories; they found me.

Each story stands on its own feet. I encourage you to read them aloud. Wrestle with the reflection questions. If you want to dig a little deeper, gather a group of friends. Read the related scripture each day for a week. Come together to listen and respond to the story. You may even want to write your own stories. If you are a teacher or a worship leader, feel free to use them (but please give credit). It will be as you dig into the stories that they will come alive for you.

I hope you will find "A Chuckle from Heaven" to be as much fun and as inspirational and as challenging for you as it was for me.

Larry

Our Story

Why do people read the Bible? Because it is far more than ancient history; it is our story, best told in first person plural, and it goes like this:

In the beginning, all was darkness and raging water. Chaos was in control. Life as we know it was not yet. But a breath hovered over the chaos, and that breath was the breath of life. This breath, which we also call "Spirit," said, "Let there be light;" and there was light.[1]

Over time, God continued to create. Land appeared as the waters receded. Microscopic creatures appeared in the water, and then fish. Earth formed plants and animals. Then humans appeared on the earth. The same breath that hovered over the chaos breathed life into our souls.

We lived in a beautiful garden, as the story goes, but there is something in our nature that is never content with what we have. We wanted more. We wanted to be like the gods. So we ate the forbidden fruit and discovered, not that we were like the gods, but that we were naked and vulnerable. We left the garden to wander the earth, till the fields, and give birth.

Some time after that, God appeared to our ancestor Abram, who was later renamed "Abraham." God promised the childless old man that his descendants would be as plentiful as the stars in the sky. God also told Abram to pack up his belongings and move to Canaan. So it was that we became a rather strange family. We were Isaac, and were easily duped by one of our sons. We were Jacob, who tricked our brother out of his inheritance and had to run away.

1

We were Joseph, spoiled rotten and hated by our brothers, sold into Egyptian slavery, and later made something of ourselves. We were terribly imperfect, the whole lot of us, but God used us anyway, and something good happened.

Our story moved to Egypt, where we became slaves in pharaoh's land. We begrudgingly listened to Moses and, after that fateful Passover, followed him across the Red Sea into the wilderness. We wandered through that arid land for forty years, following a pillar of cloud by day and a pillar of fire by night. We complained about being thirsty. Then we complained about being hungry. We worried when Moses was gone too long. We forgot who our God was and built for ourselves a golden calf. We stumbled and grumbled and basically found wilderness living to be hard going. But we also discovered that the wilderness places of our lives are places of growth and new beginnings. We formed a new society based on a new set of understandings. Our number one rule was, "There is no other god but God."[2] Everything else followed after that, including the command to care for one another. We entered the wilderness as freed slaves. We left the wilderness a new people.

Moses died, and we followed Joshua as we crossed the Jordan River into the Promised Land. These were years of conquest as we settled into our new space. Our Promised Land was a land of milk and honey, which was a way of saying it was a land of both hardship and plenty. We lived as twelve separate tribes for a long time, coming together whenever we were threatened by enemy forces. We left it to a series of powerful judges like Deborah and Gideon to make the big decisions for us.

The day came when we looked around and saw that our neighboring nations were all very strong, and they all had kings. We decided we wanted a king too. Saul was the first, and then came David and, after that, Solomon. David was the greatest of the three. He brought peace to our land, consolidated our tribes into a nation, and promoted the worship of one God. Solomon was the richest. He built our great Temple and constructed some magnificent buildings, although he did it on the backs of slave labor.

When Solomon died, our great nation split in two, with Israel to the North and Judah to the South. We entered a long period of decay.

We began to worship all sorts of other gods. We made poor treaty choices with other nations. Prophets came along to warn us that we were sliding down a slippery slope to destruction. We chose not to listen. In the end, we were defeated. Our northern kingdom of Israel was annihilated by Assyria. Some years later, the great Babylonian army besieged our southern kingdom. We in the South were captured and became prisoners of war in a strange land some 600 miles away from home.

We lived in exile for 40 years. Babylon – near the place of our captivity - was a wealthy city, full of enticements. Some of us simply let go of the past and melted into this new culture. The rest of us remained in our encampment and pined for home. We believed God had abandoned us. In fact, we believed God's home was literally in the great Temple in Jerusalem. When the Temple was destroyed, God was destroyed with it. To our great surprise, it didn't turn out that way at all. God entered our exile with us.

We returned home a full generation later. We rebuilt our Temple, but life was never quite the same. The Greeks conquered us and, later, the hated Romans came to town. We longed for a Messiah, someone who would rescue us from our plight and take us back to the days of David's dynasty.

We found our Messiah in Jesus of Nazareth, but he was not what we expected. His kingdom was not like that of David. It was not marked by territorial boundaries. It included all God's people, and it was recognized through acts of justice and compassion. What is more, our Messiah did not mount a throne but a cross. Then, most amazing of all, came resurrection. We discovered that God can overcome all darkness, even the darkness of the grave. We discovered that the evil of the world is never more powerful than the goodness of God. We discovered that abundant life is not only possible, but promised.

We came together after that to form a community of faith. At first, we were simply called people of "The Way." Later we came to be called "Church." We cared for one another and those around us. Through men like Barnabas and Paul, we began to get the word out. Others began to join us, even in the face of severe persecution. We talked about Jesus, and tried to sort out what his experience meant to us. Some of us even wrote his story down.

Unlike almost any good book, our story has no ending, just a series of new beginnings. Through it all, through all the ups and downs of human history and our personal history as well, our story is one that finds its footing in the God who keeps promises and who honors those promises with the words, "I will be with you always."[3]

[1]Genesis 1:3
[2]Deuteronomy 6:4
[3]Matthew 28:20

Reflect:

What part of this story was new for you?

What surprised you?

What did you already know?

What questions do you have?

The Garden

(Genesis 3)

Perhaps the story began something like this:

The children asked:
"Why does Daddy work so hard?"
"Why does Mommy hurt so much when she has a baby?"
"Why do snakes crawl in the grass and scare us?"

These were tough questions for any parent, but the old ones were smart enough to point the questions in the direction of deeper truth. They started by saying, "Once upon a time..."
Back in the days when life was perfect, humans and animals could communicate. They all lived together in a wonderful garden; lived as innocents, until that conversation.
One day, when everything was just perfect, the serpent saw the woman standing in the garden. The four-legged serpent was a wily old creature, so he crept over to the woman and asked a simple question:
"Did God tell you that you cannot eat the fruit from these trees?"
"Oh no," she answered. "We can eat the fruit from any tree except that tree. God said that, if we touch that tree, we will die." That wasn't exactly true. They could touch the tree; they just couldn't eat its fruit.

Why do you suppose she felt she had to stretch God's

7

laws? Why do we?

The serpent chuckled a little, and eased her over toward that tree. She looked at it again, and she repeated, "God told us not to eat." Only, she was a little less certain this time.

The serpent said:
"You know God is not really telling the truth.
"You can eat all you want, and you won't die.
"In fact, if you eat it, you will know as much as God does.
"You will even be like God."
The woman was hooked.

> *The woman was hooked, just as we would be. After all, who among us does not spend a great deal of energy trying to be like the gods? Don't we have a fundamental desire to be self-sufficient, not needing anyone's help, including God's? Don't we want to be in control and in charge of our own destiny? Don't we want to be powerful enough to direct the activities of our corner of the world? Don't we want to be knowledgeable enough to make decisions and know for certain we have made the right choices? Who among us wouldn't want to be like the gods, at least for a few days?*

She was hooked, and she - quite literally - took the bait.
She picked the fruit (which was not an apple, by the way, but perhaps a fig). She ate it, and enjoyed every bite. Her husband was right beside her all this time, which makes you wonder what he was doing. He saw how much she liked the fruit. When she picked some for him, he ate it too – and enjoyed it as much as she did.

> *So it was that they committed their first sin - and ours as well. The sin wasn't in eating the fruit; it was in trying to be like God. Who can blame them, really? How many of us try to eat that same fruit?*

8

Knowing all about good and evil brought a huge surprise. Suddenly, both of their eyes were opened. The woman and man looked at each other as if for first time, and found out they were naked. As anyone knows, when you're naked you're pretty vulnerable. They didn't like their vulnerability, so right then and there a new word entered our human vocabulary: Shame.

The woman and man chose not to face vulnerability. They decided to cover it up instead. They further decided to make themselves some new clothes. One story has it that they went to all the trees in the garden and asked each one to give them leaves for protection. No tree wanted to participate in their sin, and all said "No!" The only one willing to donate leaves was the fig, the one from whom they received the forbidden fruit.

The problem was that fig leaves were prickly and scratchy and terribly uncomfortable. So, there they were; clothed with fig leaves, itching and scratching as if they had full-body poison ivy, trying to cover up their vulnerability.

That evening the woman and man heard God's footsteps as God took a nightly stroll through the garden. By then their bodies were rubbed raw by scratchy fig leaves; their souls were raw from embarrassment. So they did what only comes natural for any one of us: They tried to hide. They tried to hide from each other; they tried to hide from God.

Perhaps they asked themselves what we sometimes ask ourselves:

"Wouldn't it be nice if God didn't know what we have done?

"Can't I just pretend nothing happened?

"Why can't I cover it up, and just make it all go away?"

They tried to hide. It was their second sin, and ours as well.

God saw through them, of course, as God has a way of doing. And God started to ask hard questions. But no one wanted to 'fess up. So they started pointing fingers.

It was their third sin, and ours as well.

9

He said, "The woman YOU gave me: SHE made me do it."

He tried to lay the blame on God as well as the woman.

She said, "Hey, it wasn't my fault. The serpent tricked me, so I really had no choice."

It was like saying, "I was deprived in childhood; therefore, I am not responsible for my actions."

Of course, God saw through it all, as God does. The man and woman did eat the fruit. They knew it. God knew it. And that was that.

Responsibility is responsibility, no matter how you color it. And consequences are consequences.

God said,

"Here is what is going to happen. You must leave the garden, and find your way in the world.

"Woman, you will bear children. In birthing, you will experience pain. But you will do it because of your desire for your husband.

"Man, you will work the soil. You will fight thorn bushes and weeds. You will sweat from exertion, and produce whatever you eat. Nothing will be handed to you.

"Serpent, you will no longer have four legs. You will crawl on the ground, and you will eat dust. Women and men will hate you. You will strike at them, and they will crush you. Now, go! All of you!"

Sin always has a price tag. Sooner or later, someone has to step up to the counter and pay the bill. It may be those who eat the fruit, or it may be handed off to future generations. But there is always a price to pay.

If you think this is the end of the story, you are wrong. There is still a postscript, an epilogue.

The man and woman began to slink away. They still wore their fig leaf wrap-arounds, so they were trying to walk and scratch at the same time. God looked at them, and God sighed. What a pitiful sight!

10

"Wait a minute," God said. "You can't go out into the world like that!" God removed their fig leaves, and God gave them clothing made out of soft fur. They had to leave the garden, but they would at least be comfortable in their journey.

This is a story about sin and its consequences, and it is more than that. It is ultimately a story about God's great love and compassion. If you look carefully, you will see it repeated around the beginning of the ADs, when God looked upon the world and realized there is no way humanity can accomplish its own salvation. Through Jesus, God showed us unconditional love as a gift with no strings attached. God only asks us to accept it.

The next time you teach a Sunday school class, or sit is a small group, or read a newspaper, and someone asks you a "why" question, don't even try to give a straight answer. Just begin, "Once upon a time, there was a garden…"

Reflect:

What were the three sins in the garden?

How do they compare with your own wishes, attitudes, and behavior?

Abraham

Lyrics: Larry F. Beman
Tune: The Gift of Love

There was a man named Abraham
Who heard the voice of the great I AM.
He left his home and family
To travel far to his destiny.

The barren desert was his home,
He spent his years condemned to roam.
Yet still he trusted God on high
To calm his fears and hear his cry.

He hoped and prayed he'd have a son;
The years slipped by and there was none.
Yet God brings life from empty tombs
And filled the ancient, childless womb.

14

Showdown at Mizpah

(Genesis 31:43-49)

No matter how much we long for the peaceable kingdom, it never seems to arrive. In the midst of ever-present tensions, tempers flare, nerves fray, and battles begin. We wonder, perhaps: Is there no hope? Is there no way out?

An ancient story in the book of Genesis is a study in conflict: what causes it and what prevents it? It is a story of two men, their prides, their prejudices, their good, and their evil. It is a tale of slowly developing conflict that reaches its flashpoint in the hill country of Gilead. The result is a showdown at Mizpah.

Imagine now that two men stand before you. Their names are Jacob and Laban. Each will tell his tale. The first will be Jacob.

Jacob:

My name is Jacob! I stand this morning on a tree-covered hill in Gilead. Laban is coming up behind me. I suppose he is as mad as a hornet after what I did to him, but he had it coming! Let me tell you about it. I think you will agree.

It all began years ago in Canaan. I was living with my father at the time. He didn't want me to marry a Canaanite woman, so he sent me to Paddam-Arram. There, I could be among my own people and pick out a wife. (Besides, I had recently tricked my brother out of his inheritance, and the atmosphere at home wasn't especially good for my health – if you know what I mean.)

I met this woman at just about the same time that I entered uncle's country. She was beautiful. Really beautiful! Her name was Rachel. I fell in love with her right away. When I found out she was my uncle Laban's daughter, I figured I was set for life. I made a deal with Laban. I would work for him for seven years. At the end of that time, I could marry Rachel.

I worked those seven years and I received no wages for my effort. I only wanted the right to marry Rachel. I loved her so much that those seven years seemed like a few days.

When the time was up, Laban held a huge wedding feast for me. I'll admit it, I got a little drunk. Actually, I was so drunk that I couldn't tell the difference between Rachel and her weak-eyed older sister Leah. Laban knew this and, in the midst of my drunkenness, gave me Leah for a wife! When I sobered up the next morning, I found Leah in my tent instead of Rachel.

I was mad! I yelled at Laban; I ranted and raved. Do you know what that old fox did? He said I could marry Rachel - if I worked for him for another seven years.

I had no choice. I worked another seven years. I worked hard too, and it paid off. Laban's herds increased. He became a wealthy man, and at my expense, I might add. Finally, I got my wish. Rachel and I were married.

Let me tell you, it is not easy being married to two women! Leah and Rachel became competitors instead of sisters, and I was the center of their rivalry. It went something like this:

Leah had four children right away, all boys. They were Reuben, Judah, Simeon, and Levi. Then she stopped having children. All this child-bearing made Rachel jealous. Rachel gave me her maid, Bilhah, and told me to have children through her. What could I do? You have to keep peace in the family, don't you? Well, Rachel had two sons through Bilhah.

It didn't work. Keep the peace, I mean. Now Leah grew jealous.

16

She gave me her maid Zilpah, and Zilpah gave birth to two more sons. Then Leah became pregnant again, and again, and again, and gave me two more sons and a daughter. Then it was Rachel's turn, and my son Joseph was born.

Now I had two wives, two maids, eleven sons, and one daughter. I began to need a little more income!

I went to Laban and asked permission to leave for my home country. He agreed, and told me to name my wages. I told him I would go through his herds and pick out the spotted and speckled lambs and goats. I would keep them, and he could have all the rest.

When the time came for the sorting, Laban tricked me again. He hid all the spotted and speckled animals in another pasture, leaving me with nothing.

I stayed a while longer and built a modest herd for myself. I began to see, however, that I was wearing out my welcome. When I built up enough assets, I left. I didn't even say goodbye.

Now he is coming after me. I wonder what is going to happen. I know one thing for certain: God promised to guide me and, no matter what, I am secure in that promise.

Laban:

I am an old man. This son-in-law has stolen from me everything I hold dear. What he has done now is the last straw, and I am going after him.

It worked well for a long time. He is my sister's son. He got into big trouble at home and came to live with me. He wanted to marry my daughter Rachel. Ah, she is a pretty girl. We made an agreement; he would work for me for seven years, and she could be his wife.

But I have an older daughter, Leah. She is not as pretty as Rachel. Weak eyes, you know. I had to take care of her too. Both girls need a husband. So, I manipulated things a little and Jacob ended up with both women.

I could see from the start that this arrangement was going to work out very well. Leah gave me grandchildren right away. Then it was Rachel's maid. And then Leah's maid. And then Leah. And then Rachel. For a while, we had a regular population explosion. I was a very happy man!

Then, Jacob asked to leave! I didn't want that. Not only did he give me grandchildren, but he was a darned good farmer. He made me a very rich man.

Well, we agreed that he could take the spotted and speckled lambs and goats and go home. Like I said, though, I didn't want him to leave. So I slightly manipulated things once again. I separated the off-color animals before he did and left Jacob with nothing. He had no choice. He had to stay with me. I was a happy man again.

Then Jacob began to trick me! I still don't know how it worked. He managed to breed the herds so that all the young were spotted, speckled or black. He claimed them for himself. His animals were strong and healthy; I was left with the runts and weaklings.

I couldn't stand still for that! I needed to get my herds back!

While I was deciding what to do, Jacob took his family and his herds and left me! He didn't even give me a chance to say goodbye to my children and grandchildren. Before he left, someone performed one last act of injustice. Someone stole my household gods. My household gods, mind you! I suspect Jacob. I don't trust that man!

Now I am going after him. Justice must be done!

I am, however, a little confused. I had a very strange dream the other night. In my dream, God told me not to say a word to Jacob, good or bad. I'm not sure how I'm going to get even, but one thing I do know: I must not disobey God.

Showdown:

The stage is now set. The two parties approach one another. Each has a serious grudge against the other. The air is thick with mutual hatred and suspicion. Such is the stuff that makes for bloodshed.

Laban approaches Jacob and lays out his grievances. Then he goes from tent to tent, ripping them apart, searching for his household gods, finding nothing.

Now Jacob is furious. He accuses Laban and screams his anger. Voices escalate.

Is it time for battle?

No.

A curious thing happens. Instead of coming to blows, they make an agreement – a covenant between them. Stones are gathered and a pillar is constructed. They call it "Mizpah," which means "watchtower." The pillar symbolizes an agreement made where each man will do what he says.

The agreement has two parts. First, the pillar becomes a territorial boundary. Neither Jacob nor Laban will ever invade the other's land. Second, the watchtower is the scene of a three-way agreement among two men and God. They say to each other, "The Lord watch between you and me, when we are absent one from the other."[1]

> *Neither Jacob nor Laban were saints. In fact, they were shysters. They played dirty tricks for personal, egotistical ends. But God watches over even the imperfect, blemished people of this world.*
>
> *Jacob and Laban were both men of faith. God was on both of their sides. Somehow, they recognized it. That one simple belief kept them from killing each other.*
>
> *Jacob lived to be an old man. His son Joseph was, in many ways, as devious as his father. Joseph was sold by his brothers into slavery and later saved the family from starvation, but that is a story for another time. Their descendents were as many as the stars in the sky and included David, Solomon, and Jesus of Nazareth.*

[1]Genesis 31:49

Reflect:

How do you typically resolve conflicts?

How does your faith impact the way you manage conflict?

You Want Me to do What?

Did you ever want to argue with God? Do you have something you need to get off your chest, but you don't think it's right to talk to God that way? Think again! Two-thirds of the Psalms are complaints! And that's nothing compared with what Moses did.

You remember Moses. He's the one who led the Hebrew people out of slavery in Egypt to the Promised Land, although it took him 40 years to cover a hundred miles or so. It didn't start out so well between him and God.

Moses was a fugitive who was wanted for murder back in Egypt. He escaped into the wilderness, met up with Jethro, and married the man's daughter. He also took care of his father-in-law's sheep. Then came that day when he was doing what shepherds do and ran into a bush that was on fire, but not burning up. He went to see what was happening and heard a Voice telling him to take off his shoes and stand barefoot on the hot sand; which he did.

Then the Voice told him about all the trouble the Hebrews were having back in Egypt. The Voice told him how the Hebrews were crying to God for deliverance and he should go back to Egypt and lead them to freedom, even though the head guy (Pharaoh) wouldn't be pleased about the whole thing.

Well, up to this point, Moses was willing to go along. After all,

21

he not only took his shoes off, but he prostrated himself in front of the bush. He knew he was in the presence of the Almighty. He just didn't care much for what God was asking him to do. So they got into an argument that lasted for the better part of two chapters in the book of Exodus. It went something like this:

God: Go back to Egypt and deliver my people from slavery.
Moses: Say what? You've got to be kidding!
God: I will be with you.
Moses: Now, if I go back there with this cockamamie story, who should I say sent me?
God: I Am Who I Am.

Moses: Right. Just suppose they don't listen to me. What then?
God: What's that in your hand?
Moses: My walking stick.
God: Throw it on the ground.
Moses: It turned into a snake! How did you do that?
God: Pick it up again.
Moses: Right. Okay. It's a stick again.

God: Put your hand inside your coat and pull it out again.
Moses: Aargh! My hand! It's covered with ugly spots.
God: Put your hand back inside your coat.
Moses: It's... better now.
God: Get my point?

Moses: I'm not a good talker. You know, I don't think of the right things to say.
God: I'll teach you.
Moses: Why don't you send someone else?
God: Shut up, and GO!

I think God doesn't mind a good argument. In fact,
I suspect God would rather we speak our minds,
talk about our discontents, argue our case, and even
whine a little than to have us run away and hide.

22

As someone once told me, "You may as well pray, because God sees what's in your heart anyway."

Reflect:

When have you questioned God?

Were your questions resolved?

What might God be asking of you
in these days of your life?

Parents

(Exodus 13:21-22)

Note: This story is best read with the grumpy voice of a discontented teen.

Parents! You can't live with them; you can't get by without them. But they do make some pretty dumb decisions sometimes. Like right now.

Here we are, out in the middle of this god-forsaken wilderness. We don't have anything to eat and I'm starving! I haven't had any food for days. We don't even know where we are going except that we are headed for some promised land somewhere. Seems to me we are just going around in circles. And all because my parents decided to listen to this guy Moses. I wonder if they know he is a murderer.

Yeah, I know. We were slaves. We had no future. Pharaoh was using us as cheap labor to build his masterpieces of architecture. I faced a career in brick making, just like my father and his father. Anybody who got out of line was executed on the spot. Baby boys were put to death right away, except for a few of us that our mothers hid from the authorities. Times were tough. I know that. But was that any worse than what we have now?

Then along came Moses. He had guts, I'll give him that. He walked right up to Pharaoh and told him to turn us loose. He even threatened bad things if his demands weren't met, like plagues of frogs and bugs and hail; stuff like that. I don't know why Pharaoh didn't have him finished off right then and there. And here's a weird thing. Moses has a speech problem, so he didn't do all the talking.

He let his brother Aaron speak for him.

Anyhow, Moses refused to take any credit for himself. He said this was all God's doing. God wanted us to be free. I'm sure Pharaoh bought that argument! After all, Pharaoh had his own gods, along with a ton of advisors. Big surprise! No matter what Moses said, we were still slaves.

Then some really wild stuff happened. Bugs and frogs and gnats plagued the country. Even the mighty Nile turned to blood! My sister really freaked! I didn't like it much either, but I didn't tell her that. Moses kept saying it was all Pharaoh's fault for not letting us go. Pharaoh wanted his cheap labor, so he just made things worse. Then came that really crazy night when we Hebrews had to put blood on our doorposts and get ready to leave quickly. I heard a lot of screaming and crying out in the city. I was scared! More scared than I've ever been. What's going to happen to us, I wondered.

Now I know. We're out here in the wilderness. Everywhere I look I see sand and rock and scrub. We walk for miles, only to camp out in the same kind of place we just left. Moses seemed so sure of himself back in Egypt. I wonder if he has any clue about where he is leading us. He keeps muttering something about a promised land and that God will get us there sooner or later. Well, my vote is for sooner. Right now I'm tired, and I'm hungry.

But can we go back home? Oh no. Some others are saying we made a big mistake. They say we were better off back where we were. But my parents? They keep telling me we have to trust. I trust that I'll be eating dirt if I don't get some food!

The funny thing is, a huge cloud showed up the other day. It stays out in front of us all the time. It's as if we're supposed to follow it. I wonder what that means.

Reflect:

What do you think you would have done if you were
wandering through the desert with Moses?

What do you do when you face an uncertain future?

Where in your life is trust important?

Pillar of Fire

Larry F. Beman

©2009

28

Pillar of Fire

night   is   long   and   I   am   we - ary.
e - ven   while   I   ask   the   ques - tion,

Bram - bles   tear   my   soul   a - part.   Then
e - ven   while   my   soul   wind   moans,   a

through   the   dark - ness   shines   a   bea - con.   A
voice   with - in   be - gins   to   whis - per:____

pil - lar   of   fire   re - stores   my   heart.
"You____   will   ne - ver   be   a - lone."

Gideon

Look at him.

Every day he stares at that ephod, that statue made of pure gold. It is supposed to point the way to God. Instead, the thing has become his god. After 40 years, our great leader has come to this.

And yet…

He has been a Godsend to our 12 tribes. For 40 years we have known peace. For 40 years we have been able to harvest our crops and raise our families without being afraid. For 40 years we have known security. What more could we ask for?

So, who is he? Is he the one who would forget who his God is, or is he the one who is faithful? How do we measure this man's legacy? He was a member of the tribe of Benjamin, the weakest of our 12 tribes. And, he was a wimp. His name is Gideon.

His story began in the spring of the year, during the wheat harvest. This was the time of year when marauding desert bandits invaded our land to steal anything they got their hands on. Gideon, along with everyone around him, spent his days hiding and doing any necessary work in secrecy. So it was that, on this day, Gideon was trying to thresh grain while hiding out in a small stone pit used to press grapes. Here, in this pit, he occasionally glanced up to see if any strangers were watching. He had nerves of, well, anything but steel.

A messenger from God appeared. A voice called Gideon by name.

Voice: Hail, mighty warrior!

Gideon: Who? Me? (He was, after all, cowering in a wine press.)

Voice: The Lord is with you!

There was silence.

Gideon: If the Lord is with me, why is all this bad stuff happening to us? Look at me. I'm down in this hole trying to separate this grain from the stalks; this chaff is sticking to me; and I am hot and dirty and I itch all over.

Voice: Go! Deliver your people from the desert bandits. I hereby commission you.

Gideon: WHAT are you talking about? My tribe is feeble! And I am the runt of the litter!

Voice: Don't worry. I will be with you.

Gideon: Right. If you're so all-powerful, show me a sign!

Gideon went into his home and brought out a big dinner: meat, cakes, and broth; the whole nine yards. The messenger said:

Voice: Put the meat and cakes on this stone. Then pour the broth over it.

Gideon did what he was told; then, yikes! Flame erupted from the rock. The meat and cakes vanished. So did the messenger.

Gideon: Oh my God! I'm in big trouble! Nobody sees the Lord face to face and lives to tell about it. Not even Moses. I know what I'll do. I'll build an altar right here. I'll call it, "the Lord is peace."

Later that night, in a dream, Gideon received his marching orders. He was to tear down a sacred pole that was used to worship another god. Gideon, the wimp, was afraid someone would see him. He snuck out of his home in the middle of the night and cut down the pole. Within a few hours, however, all fingers pointed to him. It took his father to bail him out. Still and all, he had done what he was told to do. Maybe this wimp had a half ounce of courage after all.

Some time after that, two vast tribes of desert marauders came together and planned a massive attack. Gideon sent word out to his people and somehow managed to raise an army of 32,000 men. Then he began to get cold feet. His conversation with God went something like this:

Gideon: God, I need a little proof that this is what you want me to do. Tell you what; I will lay a wool fleece on the threshing floor tonight. If, in the morning, there is dew on the wool and nowhere else, I'll know I'm doing the right thing.

And that's what happened. But Gideon wasn't satisfied:

Gideon: Pardon me, God, but I need one last little sign. Let's do the same thing all over again. This time, let there be dew on the ground but not on the wool.

Once again, that's what happened. Gideon got the point. He took his troops onto the mountain where they could see the marauders down in the valley. There were so many enemy soldiers that they couldn't even be counted. Someone wrote that they were as thick as the sand on the seashore. Gideon set about the task of developing a battle plan. God, however, had a different strategy in mind:

Voice: You have too many soldiers, Gideon.
Gideon: What are you talking about? I need as many as I can get.
Voice: If you win this battle with all these soldiers, you'll think it was your doing. Here's what I want you to do.

Following instructions, this time without argument, Gideon sent home any soldier who was terrified and trembling. Of these men, 22,000 decided that going home was a great idea. Gideon was left with 10,000 troops. God wasn't satisfied.

Voice: You still have way too many. Take them down to the stream to get a drink of water. Watch what they do. Keep anyone who laps the water with their tongue like a dog. Send home anyone who scoops up the water with their hand.

Of the remaining men, 9,700 scooped the water into their hands. Now Gideon was left with 300 troops to face a massive army of invaders. Then God spoke again:

Voice: Looks good to me! Go for it!

Gideon needed a serious plan, and he came up with a good one. He divided his soldiers into three companies and gave everyone a trumpet, a clay jar, and a torch. Then, in the middle of the night, he ordered the soldiers to circle the enemy encampment. At his signal, every man smashed his jar, held his torch high, blew on his trumpet, and shouted, "For the Lord and for Gideon."

It worked. The marauders couldn't see who had actually surrounded them and believed they were being attacked by a monstrous army that outnumbered them by a wide margin. Terrified, they fled for the desert. The battle was over before it began.

You can guess what happened after that. Gideon returned home to a hero's welcome. They wanted to anoint him king right then and there. Gideon refused, saying there could only be one ruler and that was God.

Life settled into a routine after that. People went to their homes to do what nomadic people do to make a living. Gideon raised his own family. Folks came to him from time to time to ask his advice, or to follow his lead when crises arose. For the most part, Gideon remained true to his God; except for the ephod.

He had it made out of pure gold made from the earrings of the defeated marauders. It weighed over 40 pounds. He took the statue to his home town. He and, frankly, the rest of us Israelites, went there to worship God through it. Over time, however, he prostituted himself to it, and the ephod took the place of God. The thing ensnared him, and it ensnared his family.

So there he is, nearing the end of a long and successful reign as leader of his people. He has made wise decisions; he has let the ephod control him. And I ask again, who is he? Is he the one who would forget who his God is, or is he who one who is faithful? How do we measure this man's legacy?

Reflect:

Why do you think the biblical storytellers told of Gideon's failings?

Why didn't they stop with his victories and simply paint him as a hero?

What does this tell you about God, your leaders, and yourself?

Singing Woman

(1 Samuel 1-2)

She walks across the rugged terrain, climbing the hills toward Shiloh. She brings with her a three year-old bull, some flour, some wine – and her son. Her toddler boy sometimes likes to walk, but more often she carries him as mothers have done throughout the eons. She walks with head held high and, as she walks, she sings.

This woman once thought God-forsaken is, instead, God-blessed. Her name is Hannah.

Once, she was the barren woman. She was childless. No matter how hard she tried, she simply could not have children. In her world, being barren was the ultimate degradation, the ultimate shame. What was worse, her husband's other wife gave birth to many children. This wife thought her fertility gave her the right to lord it over Hannah. She constantly belittled, provoked, and irritated on matters great and small. The household atmosphere was nearly as devastating for Hannah as her inability to give birth. She spent her days in silent screams. If people were geography, she was a rainless wasteland.

She was, and is, married to a good man. Through the years, he offered support and compassion. He tried to tell her that she mattered to him and that she was special, no matter what. Frankly, it didn't help. Once he even dared ask if he wasn't worth more than 10 sons. Her silent answer was, "No!"

Each year, the family trekked north through the hill country to bring meat sacrifices and to worship at the sacred site at Shiloh. The Ark of the Covenant, where God resided, was there. After the sacrifice, the meat was portioned out to members of the family. Hannah received a double portion as a measure of her husband's affection, but she could not eat. She simply stared at the food and wept. She was both barren and bereft.

One year after the sacrifice, Hannah left the dinner table and sobbed her way to the sacred site. Old Eli the priest was sitting by the entrance, but she paid no attention to him. She simply stood at the doorway and wept. Through her tears, she begged God to give her a son. "If you will give me a son," she cried, "I will give him back to you. He will serve you as a nazirite[1] for the rest of his life."

Eli saw her and thought she was drunk. He tried to chase her away. "You drunk! You're making a spectacle of yourself! Why don't you go home and sober up?" She turned to face him. Through her sobs she answered, "Sir, I am not drunk. Please don't see me as a worthless woman. I get enough of that already. I am just so… I am just so troubled."

Eli, brought up short, answered with a blessing, "Go in peace. May God grant you your deepest desire."

She went home to her family.

Today, she returns to Shiloh, carrying her son on her hip. She talks to the toddler as she walks along. She tells him how he was born, and that he is God's great gift to her. She tells him how much she loves him. She tells him how much his father loves him, and how the man trusts her enough to go along with her plan. She tells him he will spend his life serving God and that she will leave him at the sacred site to be trained by Eli. He doesn't understand; he is far too young, but she tells him any way.

She tells him, and she sings.

She sings of the greatness of God, and her song ripples beyond her family to include her promised-land-people. She sings of the ways God is a God of great and surprising reversals. She sings of the impoverished being raised from the dust, and of the needy being lifted of out the ash heap of life's despair. She sings of barren needs replaced and emptiness filled. "There is no Holy One like the LORD," she sings. "There is no rock like our God."[2]

She sings her way to Shiloh, this once thought God-forsaken woman, and in her singing gives birth to a fresh tomorrow.

[1]A nazirite was a man whose life was dedicated to God, either for a specified period or for a lifetime. While a nazirite, no razor could ever touch his hair; he could never approach a dead body, even that of a family member; and he could not drink intoxicating beverages.
[2]1 Samuel 2:2

Reflect:

When have you felt barren in your soul?

Have you felt the power of answered prayer?

Where do you find yourself in this story?

Eli

(1 Samuel 1-2)

What am I going to do with a *toddler*? I am an old man. I never had anything to do with child-raising. I gave that job to my wives. Now, today, this woman from down south brings me this little boy and tells me she is keeping a promise.

Maybe she made a promise, but I did not!

Let me introduce myself. My name is Eli. I am the priest who watches over the sacred site here at Shiloh. The holy Ark of the Covenant is here. This is the place where God resides. I am also a judge over Israel. I settle disputes from time to time. I take charge if a national crisis appears. I do not have child care in my job description.

Besides, I didn't do so well with my own family. I have two sons, and they are both rotten to the core. I always hoped one of them would assume my position one day but, frankly, it would be a travesty. They already embezzle meat from the sacrifices, and they obviously have no regard for the holiness of this place. No, I did not do well with my own sons; what makes anyone think I will do better with this child?

Yes, I remember the woman and her family. They are religious people, and they show up here every year or so. They bring their sacrifices, they worship, and they go home. I always thought there was something wrong with the woman, though. She never seemed happy. She never brought any children with her either, but that was none of my business. I did what was asked of me, and they went their way.

One night a couple years back, I was sitting at the entrance to the sacred site. I wasn't doing anything special, just enjoying the day. This woman came to the entrance, and just stood there. Tears ran down her face, and she was muttering under her breath. I thought she was drunk. That happens here. People eat the meat from the sacrifice and drink too much wine. Sometimes they get blubbering drunk and end up here. I chase them away. That's what I tried to do with this woman. I told her to go home and sober up. She talked back to me and told me she wasn't drunk, just deeply troubled. I gave a blessing, and she left.

I didn't think any more about it; until today.

Today she showed up again. This time she was all smiles. She told me her prayers were answered and God gave her a son. She said, "Remember when I was here before? I asked God for a son. I promised that I would give him back so he could be raised as a nazirite. He would spend his life in God's service. Well, God answered my prayers. So here he is. His name is Samuel."

Then she handed me this toddler, and she left.

She's happy; she's even singing. That's fine for her, but what about me? What do I do now? I can do prayers. I can solve problems. I can even lead a nation if I have to. Instant fatherhood is not in my skill set! Does he eat regular food? Is he sleepy? Can he talk yet? What does he like to do? How do I teach him the ways of God?

What do I do with this child? Help!

Reflect:

When have you received an unexpected "blessing?"

What did you do?

When has your comfort zone needed to expand?

When about now?

The First King

(1 Samuel 8-31)

You, my sword bearer, you see what is happening, don't you? The enemy is approaching. My sons have already been killed. Soon it will be my turn.

I – never – wanted – to – be – king! Doesn't anybody get that? The fact is, Samuel the king-maker didn't want me to be king either. He didn't want *anybody* to be king. He said there's only one king, and that's God. Why should we be like the other nations, he asked? We're different, he said. Well, one good reason is that the other nations are mighty powerful and were beating the tar out of us. In the end, people put so much pressure on Samuel that he caved in. Here's what happened.

It's a little known fact that I was a farmer. When the time came to choose a king, Samuel got all our 12 tribes together at Mizpah. Then they cast lots. You remember, don't you, why they cast lots? It meant no human was making the choice about who would be king. God was doing the choosing. One by one, tribal representatives came forward. One by one, the cast lots dismissed them; until it came time for my tribe, called Benjamin. We were chosen. Then, one by one, members of my family stood for the reckoning. Again, all were dismissed; until the lots were cast once more, and I was selected.

I was hiding in the baggage at the time, and they couldn't find me; which was exactly what I wanted. I didn't want the job. So the people prayed, and the God who sees everything knew where I was. And that was that. When I stood up, I was taller than anyone there, which made Samuel say there was no one like me. And everyone shouted "Long live the king!" Thanks a lot.

Samuel the king-maker and I never did get along. I don't know if he was jealous of me or what, but he was always in my face telling me I did something wrong. Like the time I led an army out to meet the Philistines. We found out the enemy troops numbered 30,000 chariots, 6,000 horsemen, and as many foot soldiers as there are grains of sand on the sea shore. My people were terrified. They hid in caves, holes, rocks, cisterns, and even graves. Samuel had told me to wait seven days until he showed up so that he could make an offering to God. I did wait, and it got harder and harder to keep my army from running away. The desertion rate grew higher by the minute. Seven days came and went, and Samuel didn't show his face. I suppose he had something better to do. Finally, I couldn't wait any longer. I made the offering myself. Then Samuel appeared, condemned me, told me I was useless as a king, and that I was done.

I had a few victories after that, but Samuel decided God told him to find another leader. It was too much, all of it. I grew more and more depressed. One day I found out Samuel had anointed David to be the next king. Perhaps you already know about him, and how he killed Goliath the giant. Did you know David is a brilliant strategist? Did you know he led a band of renegades for a while? Did you know I tried to catch him? Unsuccessfully, I might add. Finally, we reached some sort of compromise. Basically, I didn't chase him any more.

In the meantime, Samuel died. You'd think that would be the end of my troubles with him, but oh no. The Philistines showed up again. I asked God for help, but didn't get any answers. I asked the prophets for help. I listened for answers in my dreams. I tried a thing called Urim that was used by priests to get yes or no answers from God. No luck. Yesterday, I disguised myself and went to a medium. In the séance, she saw an old man rising out of the ground. You're right. It was Samuel. Samuel condemned me. Told me I disobeyed God throughout my reign. Told me my sons and I would die today.

I guess he was right after all. An arrow has found me. I'm hurt and I'm bleeding. The enemy approaches. You, my sword bearer, you see what is happening, don't you? I don't want it to be said that the Philistines killed me. Take your sword, and kill me. It is my final order. You will not obey? Then, I must fall on my own weapon. Now, finally, it will be over.

I never wanted to be king.

Reflect:

Have you ever taken on a role that was uncomfortable for you?

What was the result?

How have you felt toward the antagonists in your life?

Do you believe you have been selected by God for something special?

Why or why not?

Michal

(1 Samuel 18-19; 25:44. 2 Samuel 3:12-17; 6:16-23)

She was Michal (pronounced mē-kal), and she was the daughter of the king. These were heady days in her world. For hundreds of years, her country was loosely governed by a series of judges. Then, almost overnight, the political world changed and Saul, her father, was anointed king.

Michal, the king's daughter, was in love with a shepherd whose name was David. Did she know that old Samuel the king-maker was disillusioned with her father? Did she know that Samuel had searched for a new leader and had found one in David? Did she know she was stepping into a minefield of hate and mistrust? Perhaps not. She was in love with this handsome young man, and that was what mattered.

Saul, however, saw David in a different light. Simply put, David was a threat. The king was terrified by enemies, real and imagined, and did everything in his power to protect his monarchy. David had to be eliminated. So Saul concocted a plan, a scheme that would bring no dishonor to himself and still accomplish his purposes.

Saul announced that he would give Michal to David in marriage. No dowry would be necessary, but he insisted on one small act of commitment. David must bring the king the foreskins of 100 enemy soldiers. Since no enemy soldier was likely to agree to this willingly, this meant David and his small militia had to attack the enemy and kill 100 men. Since this was an impossible task, David would certainly be killed and the threat to Saul's reign would be ended.

Somehow, David turned the tables on Saul. The requirement was met, and Michal became David's first wife.

Saul grew more and more paranoid after that. One day David played the lyre to ease Saul's anxiety. Saul suddenly jumped up and tried to skewer David with a sword. Instead of running away, David went home. Michal was more astute than David this time. She saw danger where he did not. Their home at that time was situated on the outside wall of the city. Michal helped David escape through a window and then deceived both the guards and her father.

Michal's life was a downward spiral from that time on. David, now safe, never sent for her. Instead, he married two other women. Saul, by way of getting revenge against David, gave her in marriage to another man who loved her deeply.

In due time, Saul died in battle and David became king. In one of his first acts, David sent troops to surround the place where Michal lived and forced her to return to be part of his harem. Michal's present husband was devastated. The man tried to persuade David to leave her with him, but it was no use. Michal became the property of the king.

Some time later, an exuberant David entered the city wearing very little clothing. This was a great day for the now-powerful man, and David danced. He danced so vigorously that – and there is no way to say this politely – he exposed himself. Michal saw what he did, and she was disgusted. She confronted him later, and their argument was bitter.

Her indictment oozed sarcasm. "My, how the king honors himself. He exposes himself to servant women in the way any vulgar male would show his manhood."

David shot back, "I'll dance in any way I choose. I shall be even more shameless. I am certain my maids saw me, and they shall hold me in very high regard!"

David had nothing more to do with Michal after that. She never bore him children and, in her world, this was her ultimate shame. In status, she became the lowest woman in the king's stable of wives.

Her tragedy was now complete. Manipulated by her father, thrown away by her husband, taken from the one man who truly loved her, Michal's story ended in heartbreak. While David's star rose, Michal's dreams were ground in the dust of history's parade.

This is not the kind of story you expect to find in the Bible. It is a tragedy without a happy ending. It makes you wonder, where was God? What happened to the moral standards expected then and now of great leaders? And, perhaps just as important, how do we treat the Michals who live in our world – those women who are abused or manipulated or cast aside?

Reflect:

What normal standards do you expect of your leaders?

Who in your world is like Michal?

How do you treat these people?

David

(David's story is found in 1 and 2 Samuel and the early chapters of 1 Kings.)

Come here, child. You are a beautiful young woman. I am glad you have been assigned to me. Wrap me in more clothes. Rub my back. Please. I am so cold. It is summer outdoors, but I cannot keep warm. My children are talking behind my back. Who will take my place when I am gone, they wonder. I suppose it's natural. After all, it won't be long now.

I spend my days remembering. I was a shepherd when I was a child, not far from here. I spent my days, and some nights too, taking care of my father's flock. It was an important job. Then Samuel came along one day, took a look at me, and decided I was to be the next king. He said I was God's choice.

I went to visit my brothers not long after that. They were in the army, fighting the enemy that came from the sea. The enemy was big and strong, and better armed than we were. When I took food to my brothers, a huge man from the other army came out into no-man's land every day with a challenge. He wanted someone from our side to fight him. Whoever won the fight won the war, and the winner got the spoils. It was a common practice in those days, and I suppose it saved lives.

I don't know why I did it, but I told everyone I would fight the giant. They told me I was crazy, but I believed I could win. I was persuasive enough that they finally gave in. First they tried to fit me with a man's armor but I looked ridiculous. I couldn't even move in that stuff. In the end, it was just me and the sling shot I used to protect my sheep. Well, you know the rest of the story.

Am I boring you, child? Do you want to hear more?

Saul was king in those days, and I married his daughter Michal. She was my first wife. Saul was often depressed and angry, so I often played my lyre for him. One day he tried to kill me, and I ran to the wilderness down near the Dead Sea. I formed a gang of other outlaws, and we were pretty successful. Saul came after me, but he was no match for us. One day he blundered into the cave where we were hiding, and I had an opportunity to kill him. Instead, I simply snuck up behind him and cut the tassel off his prayer shawl. After all, he was God's anointed king and I could not assassinate a man like that. I told him what I had done, and we formed a sort of truce.

I took over as king when Saul was killed while fighting the Philistines. I had several wives by then, and some children as well. I guess… No, I know. My special gift was my leadership in battle. I could outmaneuver any enemy, and I did. Ultimately, our land knew peace and, with peace, came prosperity. I consolidated the 12 tribes and moved our headquarters to Jerusalem. It was a good choice, because none of the tribes claimed Jerusalem as theirs.

Are you sure you don't mind listening to an old man ramble on?

While I was good at being a king, I wasn't so good at family life. You heard about my beloved Bathsheba, didn't you? Well, I won't go into that. I did something terrible and we all paid a price for it. That wasn't all. Most people don't know the rest of my family story. My oldest son, Amnon, fell for the daughter of one of my other wives. He tricked both her and me, and he seduced her. Her brother Absalom wanted revenge, and got it by killing Amnon. I don't know if this was the beginning of all the trouble or whether it goes back farther than that.

What I do know is that Absalom made plans to depose me. It got so bad that I had to run away for a time. As I said, however, I was always a good soldier. Absalom's followers were killed in battle. My general found Absalom with his hair caught in a tree and executed him. I got my throne back, but at a terrible price.

You brought me another blanket. Thank you. I do shake from the chill.

54

When I looked back, I saw all that I had done. I had even built some fine buildings here in Jerusalem. But I wanted to do more for my God. I wanted to build a house for God. I put the plans in place, just as I did for everything else I had done. But my best advisor, Nathan, came to me. I should tell you about Nathan sometime. He was the one man who dared to stand up to me. Well, he told me God spoke to him and told him that the house of the Almighty should not be built by a man whose hands were soaked in blood. I listened to him, for I knew his words were true and faithful.

Well, that's my story. Or at least some of it. Can you play the lyre? Would you play a song I once wrote? They do offer some comfort. The words go like this:

The Lord is my shepherd, I shall not want.
He makes me lie down in green pastures;
He leads me beside still waters;
He restores my soul.[1]

[1]Psalm 23:1-3

Reflect:

Read Psalm 23 several times.

What might this psalm have meant to David during the various stages of his life?

What words or phrases stand out for you?

Sarah

(The Psalms)

Sarah was 98 years old the year she faced cancer surgery. We all knew this was going to be a tough fight for her, and we worried. Sarah, apparently, did not.

Sarah grew up in St. Eustatius in the Virgin Islands. The rule in her family and her faith tradition was that she went to church on Wednesdays and Sundays. On Wednesdays, she was to memorize a scripture verse. On Sundays, she was to memorize both a scripture verse and a hymn.

I met Sarah when she was in her early 80s. As a pastor, I visited her home every month or so, sometimes to bring communion, but more often just to talk. With her unique accent and the twinkle that always seemed to be in her eye, I found these visits to be incredibly refreshing. I am certain our times together did more for me than they did for her.

Very often on these visits, Sarah remembered a hymn from her childhood days and sang it to me. She always prefaced it by asking, "You know this one, don't you?" I had three problems. First, I couldn't understand her words through her thick accent. Second, she sang in a monotone. Third, I had never heard the hymn in my whole life. She always gave me a look of mock disgust and we moved on to a different

57

topic.

Sarah entered the hospital on the day before her surgery. I went to see her around seven the next morning, expecting to find her lying in bed waiting for the appointed hour. Instead, she was sitting cross-legged in the hospital bed talking to her two daughters. She was bright and cheerful and enjoying our company.

In my best pastoral voice, I asked how she was doing. She said she was doing just fine. I asked if she slept at all. That was when she surprised me.

Sarah told me she did not sleep. Instead, she spent the night repeating the scriptures she remembered from her childhood and silently singing the hymns that were embedded in her memory. Then she commenced singing, once again reminding me that I should know the hymn and once again looking disgusted that I had never heard it before. I had better luck with the scriptures, and we all remembered them together as we spoke in unison. The Psalms were her favorites: "The Lord is my shepherd."[1] "I lift my eyes to the hills."[2] "God is our refuge and strength, a very present help in trouble."[3] No scripture ever read in worship was more sacred than what we remembered in that early morning hour before the nurses arrived.

Sarah survived the surgery and lived for another five years. I continued to visit her and also continued disremembering the hymns she sang, but I never forgot the power of a psalm remembered in the middle of a fearful night.

[1]Psalm 23
[2]Psalm 121
[3]Psalm 46

Reflect:

What hymns or psalms have a hold on you?

What words from the psalms might you want to remember
when you face the trials of your life?

Be Still

Psalm 46
(for Barbara)

Larry F. Beman

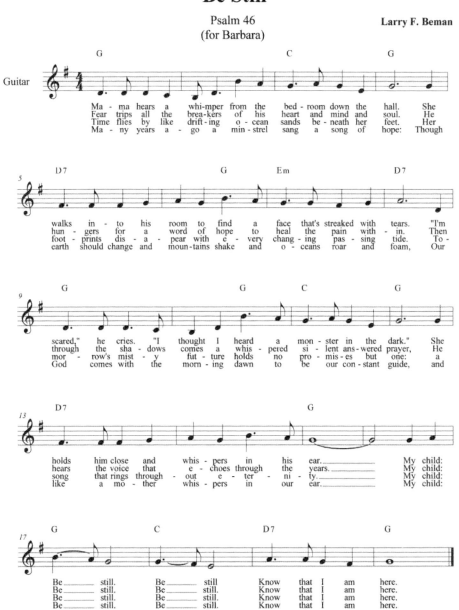

©2009

Be Still, and Know

(1 Kings 19, Mark 1)

"Shh.
    Be still.
    Be still, and know…
    Be still and know - that I am God!"[1]

It happened this way.

The prophet Elijah was in big trouble. He had stepped on the toes of some mighty powerful people. First, he confronted the king and held the man up as a numbskull who led the nation into turmoil. Then he made 450 religious leaders look completely foolish. This was not in his best interest, since the religious rulers were faith counselors to Jezebel, the king's wife. All this infuriated Jezebel, and she sent word that she would get Elijah if it was the last thing she did. So, Elijah did what comes naturally. He ran away.

First, he ran into the wilderness. He stayed there for 40 days, wishing he could die (Of course that was the same wish the king's wife had, but it came out a little differently when Elijah said it). Then he ran for another 40 days and nights until he found a new hiding place in a cave on a mountain.

One day, he stepped outside his cave to witness a mighty display of God's power. While watching, he waited to hear the voice of God.

A tremendous wind storm tore at the mountain and split rocks apart. Then an earthquake shook the foundations of the earth. After the earthquake came fire. But Elijah did not find God in the wind, or in the earthquake, or in the fire.

After all that, the Bible says, came something else. And that something else was the sound of sheer silence. And in that silence Elijah found the God he had been waiting for.

"Shh.
Be still.
Be still, and know...
Be still and know - that I am God!"

Fast forward a few hundred years. It happened this way.

Busy days were typical for Jesus, and this one was no different. It started with a walk along the shores of Galilee, where he came across a group of fishermen. Come with me, he shouted to them, and I will teach you to fish differently. So they did. Then he walked alongside them back into Capernaum, their home town. He went into the synagogue and spent time teaching. He astounded his listeners, for he sounded like he knew what he was talking about. A man with what they called an unclean spirit confronted him and was healed. And this was just the beginning.

He went home with Peter and found Peter's mother-in-law sick in bed. He eliminated her fever and she got up and made dinner. By nightfall, the whole community was buzzing. People stood outside his door, waiting for a word of healing or hope or whatever else he might offer. It took hours.

When everyone was gone, he finally got a few hours sleep. But he apparently knew that he couldn't be faith-filled simply through busy-ness. Early the next morning, he slipped out of town to be alone. The Bible says simply, "and there he prayed."[2] It was the beginning of a new day.

"Shh.
Be still.
Be still, and know...

64

Be still and know - that I am God!"

Fast forward about 2,000 years. It happened this way.

They walked the beach at sunrise. It was an annual tradition. They escaped the cold, cruel March of the Northeast for the ocean shores of north Florida. They escaped as well the tyranny of schedules and things needing to be done and spent time in re-creation and re-generation. And so they walked.

The beach was unoccupied at this time of day except for gulls and pelicans preparing for breakfast. Footprints from the previous day were washed away by high tide. The only sound, the overarching sound, came from the breakers cleansing the shoreline. The world of the seashore was waiting expectantly for a triumphal entry.

Far out on the eastern horizon, a dash of color glinted against the early morning darkness. Then a few rays leapt out of the ocean, heralds announcing the advent of the spectacular. The walkers stopped walking and stared as the sun made its grand entrance. One moment the sun was sleeping in the ocean depths; the next moment it was fully awake and rising quickly into the morning sky.

They stared in silence and awe at the moment of rebirth. Nothing in all creation could match what they had witnessed once again. Then, quietly, she began to sing: "O Lord my God, when I in awesome wonder…"[3]

"Shh.
Be still.
Be still, and know…
Be still and know - that I am God!"

[1]See Psalm 46:10
[2]Mark 1:35
[3]from "How Great Thou Art

Reflect:

Where do you go when you need to be still?

Where do you need a sense of stillness in your life?

What will you do to make it happen?

$Exile!$

I was driving through the country with my 92 year-old mother. Something she saw through the car window triggered a story from her past. After telling her tale, she was quiet for a moment. Then she said, "I don't know what we'd do without our memories."

Back in the BCs, the Hebrew people echoed the same thought. Their great city of Jerusalem had been destroyed by the great Babylonian army, and with it, their dreams. They were in exile in and around the great city of Babylon, 600 miles from home, and had been there for the better part of 40 years. During these long decades, many of them were seduced by the bright lights and the grandeur of the city; they simply vanished into the fabric of the surrounding culture. The rest stayed together, and they remained faith-filled. Together, they looked to their past for meaning and direction.

Imagine two men gathered in front of their tents along one of the canals that brought water from the Euphrates into Babylon. They talk, they dream, and they remember.

Reuben: Good day Mordecai, my old friend. It is good to see you again.

Mordecai: It is good to see you as well. It is almost sundown and time for the Sabbath. Soon we shall be together again. Soon we shall worship. Soon we shall sing the songs of old. Soon we shall remember.

Reuben: It is important to remember. It has been so long and, if we did not gather like this, our memories would fade like the leaf that the wind blows away. Maybe someday we can go home again. Maybe someday we can go to our Temple again. But for now, we do the best we can.

Mordecai: They were great times, weren't they? David and Solomon, our great kings. We knew peace and prosperity like never before.

Reuben: Yes, but we cannot forget the other times; like the days after Solomon died. One of his sons threatened to turn some of our people into slaves. They revolted and went off to the North to form their own kingdom. After that breakaway, nothing was ever the same.

Mordecai: Yes, of course. It's hard to remember all the names of all the 20 kings after the split. Asa and Jehoshaphat. And I remember Zedekiah, our last king. Some of them were okay; others, well…

Reuben: I know what you mean. Do you remember Josiah and the reform movement? He tried to bring us back to a life based on the Torah. It worked for a while, but he died fighting the Egyptians. His son took over and everything went down hill.

Mordecai: People tried to tell us we were heading down a slippery slope. I still remember some of what they said. Jeremiah warned us. Joel called us drunkards. Isaiah came right out and promised destruction. Mostly, we didn't listen.

Reuben: Actually, we shuddered when they showed up.

Mordecai: But all they wanted was for us to pay attention to what is important. They just wanted us to quit worshipping the wrong gods and to quit making alliances with the wrong nations. They just wanted us to quit focusing on the rich and powerful. They just wanted us to, you know, like Micah said, do justice, love kindness, and walk humbly with our God.

Reuben: And mostly, we did just the opposite. That's how we ended up where we are.

Mordecai: Looking back, it seems we did well as long as we followed in the ways of God. We got in trouble when we lost our sense of morality and faithfulness.

Reuben: Do you think God will ever listen to us again? Do you think we will be prisoners forever?

Mordecai: I don't know. After all these years, I confess I'm getting discouraged.

Reuben: Me too. I know one thing. We need to keep our memories alive. We must never forget. And Lord help us if we don't remember the why as well as the how.

Mordecai: Come. It is time to gather as a synagogue. My friend told me a man says he has a new message from God. I wonder... Well, let's just go and hear for ourselves.

Reflect:

What have you learned from your past?

The ancient Hebrews believed their country's fortunes rose and fell depending on their faithfulness and their ability to live justly.

Do you believe this is still true? Why, or why not?

Last Thoughts

(The book of Esther)

Mordecai! I spit on him! Who is he but a lousy Jew? He should be climbing the stairs to the gallows, not me! I am Haman,[1] the king's chief of staff! How was I to know?

And this new queen, Esther. She betrayed me! She is a gorgeous woman. I never knew she would dare…

Oh, I remember that day. I was just appointed to my new position. I was proud. I was in charge. Everyone bowed down to me. They were smart enough to bend in the face of power. Everyone except Mordecai! That worm! He refused to show me the respect I deserved. Every day it was the same thing. I walked around the outskirts of the palace, and it was as if I was parting the sea. People were intimidated. I loved it! And Mordecai just sat there.

It was beneath me to single him out, so I decided to annihilate all the Jews in our land. I made elaborate plans and got king's approval. I cast the pur, like dice, and set a time for the genocide to begin.

I don't know where I went wrong.

I was invited to a banquet with just the king and queen. What an incredible honor! I went home to tell everyone my good news. I let everyone around me know how rich I was. I showed off my sons. I explained my rise to power. And, to top everything off, I announced my banquet invitation. Then I said the only thing in my way was that Jew Mordecai. My wife suggested that I build a 70 foot high gallows and have the man hanged from it. It was a great plan! How could I go wrong?

On the day of the banquet, the king asked me what he could do for someone he wanted to honor. Well, who could he honor except for me? I told him to clothe the man in royal robes, let the man ride the king's horse, put the royal crown on the man's head, and parade the man around town. Then the king told me to do those very things for that Jew Mordecai! How was I to know that miserable Mordecai once thwarted an assassination plot? I was mortified. I covered my head and slunk home.

Everything went well at the banquet until tonight. The king, queen, and I were drinking good wine when the king told Queen Esther he would grant her any favor. Esther answered that a plot was underfoot to annihilate both her and her people. I didn't know she was a Jew also! How could I? The king asked her who the culprit was. She pointed to me!

The king got up and went to his garden to think. I panicked! I went to Esther to convince her to change her mind. I threw myself on the couch where she was lying. Just then the king came back into the room. He saw me and thought I was about to molest his wife.

So, here I am, climbing the gallows steps. I had a brilliant future. Mordecai destroyed it all. If I had one wish, if I could do just one thing differently, I would go back in time and kill that miserable man with my bare hands! After all, he's only a Jew! What difference would it make?

[1]Pronounced Hā-man.
[2]Esther 4:14

Reflect:

For a queen to approach a king without being bidden was to risk execution.

Early on, Esther was reluctant to stand up for her people. Mordecai, the man who raised her, argued, "Who knows? Perhaps you have come to royal dignity for just such a time as this."[2]

What does this say to you at this moment in your life?

Who are the disenfranchised in your world?

When and where is it important to stand up for the right even in the face of potential consequences?

The Sailor

(Jonah)

Hey! You talkin' to me?

Yeah, I'm a sailor. Yeah, I been to Tarshish a time or two. What do you wanna know?

Jonah? No. Doesn't ring a bell. Wait. You mean the guy who went overboard in the storm? Okay, I remember now. You want to know about him? I'll tell you, but you gotta know I didn't have nothin' to do with it. Nothin'. You understand?

This Jonah, he comes to the ship just before we set sail. Looks scared, like he's runnin' away or somethin'. Buys passage for Tarshish. Hey, we can always use an extra buck or two.

A couple days later, this big storm comes up. Now, I ain't scared of much, I've been goin' to sea most of my life. But this storm is different. The wind pounds the sails. Waves are crashing over the bow. We can't do nothin' to help ourselves.

We starts prayin' and calling out to our gods. Maybe one of 'em hears us, you see. Then we throw cargo overboard. Lighten the ship and we won't sink, maybe. Meanwhile, this guy Jonah is sleepin' like a newborn baby. What's with him, we wonder. The captain, he goes to this guy and wakes him up. "Pray to your god," the captain orders. "Maybe your god will save us."

Well, nothin's workin'. So we wonder who's to blame. You see, if anything bad happens, it's gotta be because somebody did something wrong and made some god mad. Only way to find out is to cast lots. You know, like dice. So that's what we do, and what do you know? It's Jonah!

We ask him what he's done. He says he's a Hebrew. Worships the Lord, he says. Now we're even more scared. We've heard about this Lord, you see. We ask him again what he's done. He tells us he's runnin' away from the Lord. Well, even I know you can't do that and git away with it.

By now the sea's really rollin', so we asks Jonah what we gotta do to him so the sea quiets down again. He says we gotta throw him overboard. Well, we don't want to do that, so we gets out the oars again and rows even harder. It doesn't work. Remember now, I didn't have nothin' to do with what happens next. Some sailors give him what he asks for. They toss him overboard.

As soon as they does that, the storm quits, and the sea's a dead calm. Now we're even more scared, so we offers a sacrifice to Jonah's Lord.

But this ain't the end of the story. Sounds crazy, but this is what I heard happened. Jonah gets swallowed up by a big fish and spends three days in the fish's belly. Must have stunk somethin' awful. Then he gets spit up onto dry land.

After that, Jonah goes and does what he was supposed to do in the first place. He goes to Ninevah, where there ain't no Hebrews like him, and he tells them they got three days to fix their ways. Kin you imagine some stranger sayin' that to you? What would you do? Probably laugh at him, that's what I'd do. But no. The king shows up, makes some pronouncement, and things change just like Jonah told them to do.

You'd think Jonah'd be happy now. Not him. He goes outside Nineveh and pouts under some shade tree. That's when Jonah's Lord shows up and chews him out. I hear it had something to do with Jonah's shade tree losin' its leaves. Then Jonah's Lord tells him to quit bellyachin'. His Lord says something like, "I have every right to care about these folks, even if they ain't Hebrews like you."

Well, that's what I know about Jonah. That answer your question? I gotta go now. I only get a day in this town, and I don't mean to spend all my time talkin', if you catch my drift. Oh, if you ever run into this Jonah, tell him what I heard. Ask him if that's what really happened.

Reflect:

When have you found yourself running away from God?

What was the result?

Jonah did not want to go to Nineveh because he thought they were unworthy of God's love.

When have you experienced similar emotions?

Immigration Reform

(The Book of Ruth)

Israel and Judah were both defeated. Residents of Jerusalem and the surrounding area were sent off for 40 long years of exile. They had plenty of time to think. They remembered what they did right and they also remembered what they did wrong. They remembered how they strayed from their trust in the one God, worshipped other deities, and allowed justice to fall by the wayside. When they returned home, they vowed to remain true to their God at all costs. As a result, their leader Nehemiah ordered ethnic cleansing. He fought with the men – even beat them and pulled out their hair – and ordered them to get rid of wives who were not Jews. No man or woman was to marry someone outside the faith. Some say this story came from that turbulent time.

Imagine now a man standing to speak to the political and religious leaders of his nation during this period of ethnic cleansing.

Gentlemen, I hear you are planning to send our foreign wives away and force our men to marry women from among our own people. I did not come here to protest your actions. I know you are trying to keep our faith pure and free from contamination by other beliefs. Instead, I must tell you a story. It begins in the days when the judges ruled the land.

She is Naomi, and her story could be our story. She walks through Bethlehem with her head held high. She is at home. She is at one with her family and with her people. It wasn't always that way.

Once she was married. She is married no longer. His name was Elimelech, which means "God is King" and they lived in Bethlehem, which means "house of bread." When the crops failed, Elimelech, Naomi, and their two sons turned away from the house of bread and moved to a foreign land. In this strange land, their sons met and married women who were not of their faith or culture.

Then tragedy destroyed Naomi's life and also her future. Her husband died, and then her two sons passed away as well. She, who depended on her men for well-being, was left with nothing. Some time later she learned that the famine was over and bread had returned to the house of bread. She decided to go home.

As Naomi prepared for her leave-taking, she told her two daughters-in-law to go back to their families. There they would find security and, most likely, re-marry. She knew she was a woman without hope for restoration. Perhaps her daughters-in-law would discover a better fate. One of the women listened to her sound advice. The other, Ruth, did not.

Ruth, the woman from a different culture, refused to be persuaded. "Don't send me back," she pleaded. "Let me go with you. I have made my commitment; don't ask me to change my loyalties. Where you go, I go. Where you live, I live. Your people are my people. Your God is my God." Love and loyalty trumped expectations, and so they turned together toward the house of bread.

Ten years had passed since Naomi left Bethlehem with her family. She caused quite a stir when she walked back into her home town. Perhaps folks were surprised to see her again. Perhaps they were upset that she brought a despised Moabite woman with her. We don't know. We do know that only the women of the town spoke to her. "Are you Naomi?" they asked.

"Don't call me Naomi," she answered. "Naomi means 'sweet' and 'pleasant.' Call me Mara. Mara means 'bitter.' God has treated me bitterly. I have been punished." With that pronouncement, an angry, discouraged, hope-destroyed woman set about the task of surviving in a community she had once left behind. It was the beginning of the barely harvest.

Now, gentlemen, I suppose you wonder why I tell this story. Perhaps you think it has nothing to do with our present situation. Please, don't try to shout me down. Let me continue. There is more.

The scene changes. Imagine a man, a respected Bethlehem landowner, sitting alongside the road. Listen while he speaks.

Heh-heh. I'm Boaz; a distant relative of Elimelech. You know, Naomi's dead husband. That's important, but I'm getting ahead of myself.

It is spring, the time for the barley harvest. A little while back I went out to my fields to see how things were going. My workers were picking the grain to bring to the threshing floor. Behind them, a woman was picking the leftovers. That's not so unusual; it happens all the time. Our laws require that we leave some behind for the poor and for people who have no land of their own.

I casually asked my workers who this woman was. It turns out she came from Moab. Now understand, we're not very fond of Moabites. But I saw something different in her. She worked all day without taking a break. In this heat, that takes stamina. I told her to stay in my fields and follow my workers. If she needed a drink, she could use the water the young men drew from the well.

Somewhere along the way I learned she was Ruth, Naomi's daughter-in-law. She left her own relations in Moab to become one of us here in Bethlehem. She gave up everything. I was impressed. I told my men not to bother her, and even to leave some extra for her.

Well, one thing led to another until one night I stayed late at the threshing floor. I ate my dinner there and had some wine to drink as well. Later, I lay down to go to sleep. She came to me that night. I won't go into what happened after that. It's just between the two of us, and it's going to stay that way.

What I will tell you is that I decided right then to do something about Ruth and Naomi's situation. If I were to marry Ruth, then Naomi would finally be restored in her relationship with our community. Even though Ruth was an alien in our midst, she proved herself worthy of anything I could offer her and her mother-in-law. I just had one sticky little problem. Another kinsman is more closely related to Naomi than I am. He has certain rights of inheritance, and I need to talk to him. That's why I'm standing alongside the road. Here he comes. Listen in if you want…

"Hello my friend. Come and sit with me a while. Let us gather 10 men around us so that we can have a little conversation. This way, everything we decide can be made legal. Now, you know Naomi, do you not? She has returned from Moab. Yes, her husband died there, as did her sons. Of course. A terrible tragedy.

"You know, did you not, that she is selling a piece of property that belonged to Elimelech? Would you like to redeem it? If not, then I will, for I come after you in the line of kinship.

"You will? Wonderful. Oh, by the way. You do know that the day you acquire the field you also acquire the Moabite woman who came home with Naomi. She was the wife of one of Naomi's sons, and you must marry her in order to maintain the dead man's legacy on this piece of land.

"Oh, you didn't know that? I'm sorry. And marrying this Moabite woman will interfere with your own inheritance? I see. That's a problem. You want me to take on the next of kin duties? In the presence of these 10 men, you have given me your sandal as a sign that I am redeeming this land?

"You 10 men? You have witnessed this agreement? You are blessing me? I hear your words: 'May the Lord make the woman who is coming into your house like Rachel and Leah, who together built up the house of Israel.'[1] Thank you."

Gentlemen, I see you are still puzzled. Why am I telling you this love story? What does it have to do with the discussion at hand? Please, one more minute. Let me finish.

Boaz did indeed marry Ruth. In due time she gave birth to a son. Naomi now had both a home and an inheritance. She was redeemed. She was restored. No longer did she call herself "Bitter." She was Naomi, the proud woman who walked the streets of the House of Bread. The child was named Obed. Obed, when full grown, was the father of Jesse, who was the father of David, our greatest king; and all because an alien woman became one of us.

So, gentlemen, we know God's ways are mysterious. I urge you to take great care in deciding who you will include and who you will exclude. Who knows? The one you expel may very well be the God-chosen man or woman sent to bring us redemption. Good day and God be with you.

[1]Ruth 4:11

Reflect:

Who do you include in your community? Who do you exclude?[1]

What is the meaning of this story for your life?

One word used often in the book of Ruth is "turn." Naomi turned toward Bethlehem. One daughter turned back.

What have been the turning points in your life?

How have they helped make you who you are?

Naomi moved from being the bitter one to again being the pleasant one.

When have you needed restoration? What happened?

On a scale of one to 10, with one being "bitter" and 10 being "pleasant," where are you in your life right now?

Heaven and Hell

Hell

The Valley of Hinnom is located near the southern wall of Old Jerusalem. The valley came to be known as Gehenna. Gehenna came to be known as another word for hell, and for good reason. In ancient times, Gehenna was the place where parents sacrificed their children to the god Molech. In the ceremony, priests beat on drums so that parents could not hear the agonized cries of their children. Later, Gehenna became the city's garbage dump. Fires burned continuously. The corpses of criminals were dumped there, along with animal carcasses. In the Sermon on the Mount, Jesus warned against being thrown into the hell of fire. The word for "hell" in the original language is "Gehenna."

Through the centuries, these original images of hell grew and mutated. Hell came seen as a place of fire where the souls of the damned are condemned to an eternity of torment. We have mostly forgotten where the image came from.

I have another image of hell. It goes like this:

Imagine you are in an airplane flying over the Atlantic (or the Pacific, or any ocean of your choice). After several hours, you reach the very center of the ocean. At that point, the plane loses altitude and slows down. A cabin door is opened. You are pulled to the door, kicking and screaming, and are pushed out.

You fall feet first into the sea, but it is not an ocean of water. Rather, it is an ocean of oatmeal; cold, lumpy, oatmeal.

You sink slowly until you reach a state of equilibrium. You try to move, but you cannot. You try to scream, but all you get is a mouth full of – you guessed it – oatmeal.

In this oatmeal sea there is no sound. There is no movement. There is no anything. And there you spend eternity.

I don't believe in hell as a physical place of fire. I believe hell is alienation; alienation from God, alienation from one another. Some people live in hell right here on earth.

By the way, the old English derivation of hell originally meant "covered" or "hidden" or "unseen."

Heaven

Yes there is.

No there isn't.

The Pharisees and Sadducees, religious leaders of Jesus' time, didn't agree on very much. They certainly didn't agree on the question of life after death. The Pharisees were on the "yes there is" side of the argument. They believed rewards would one day be handed out. Good people would finally get their reward; and the evil folks would get their comeuppance for once and for all time. They also liked what the writings in the book of Daniel said a few hundred years earlier.[1] The Sadducees were on the "no there isn't" side. They said the Torah (the five books of the Law) doesn't mention life after death, so there is no such thing.

Jesus came down on the Pharisees' side of the argument. While he was more interested in how God's people behave in the here and now, he also made mention of life beyond life. Like the time on the cross when he welcomed the thief into paradise.

The Bible doesn't say much about what heaven is like, except that it isn't cold oatmeal. I think I know.

Heaven is like being a child again. You are lying in bed with your covers wrapped all around you. You are cozy and warm. Your grandma is sitting on the bed, and she is reading your favorite bedtime story to you. You have picked a story with lots of pages so that she will stay with you for a long time. You know she loves you, and you love her right back.

If hell is alienation, I believe heaven is intimacy; intimacy with God, intimacy with one another. Some people live in heaven right here on earth. After all, why wait?

[1]Daniel 12:2

Reflect:

What are your images of heaven and hell?

When have you lived in either situation?

Where are you right now?

A Baby's Crying

Larry F. Beman

©2009

Jacob's Friend

(Matthew 1:18-25)

Hey Jacob, wait up. Let me walk with you a while. Yes, thank you. I am well. In fact, it is a beautiful day to be alive, don't you think?

It is good to talk sometimes, especially among friends. And I consider you to be one of my best friends, which is why I want to talk.

I am worried about your boy Joseph. He is all grown up now. He has learned a good trade working with his hands, and he will be able to provide someone with a good home. He has good standing in our little community. At least, he did until now.

What has he done? I don't understand.

We all know Mary. She grew up here. We all know Anne and Joachim, her parents. They are good people. We never thought Mary would do this thing. What a tragedy! And here she was engaged to your Joseph. Everything was looking good.

Now we find out she is pregnant. No one knows who the father is. Do you know, Jacob? I'm not being nosy or anything, just curious. You can tell me. I'm your best friend. I won't tell anyone. I am only asking because I worry about you.

Joseph has choices. You know that. This engagement is legal, and it is binding. You know that too. She has betrayed him. He can have her stoned to death. He can humiliate her. He can even divorce her quietly if he doesn't want to make a fuss. He has to do something to say this is all wrong, doesn't he?

Now I hear he is going ahead with plans to marry this woman. She is going to have this baby and it isn't even his child. What was he thinking? Did he have a bad dream or something? Jacob, I worry. What will happen? People are talking, you know. Today I heard talk that the emperor has ordered a census and everyone has to go to their home town to be counted. Does this mean he has to go all the way to Bethlehem? Is she going too? What is happening with him?

Jacob, why aren't you saying anything?

Why are you smiling?

Reflect:

If you were Joseph's father, how would you have responded to the news that your son was going to remain committed to Mary?

What If...?

(Luke 2:1-20)

This messes with my mind.

My traditional image of the story of Jesus' birth goes something like this:

Mary and Joseph were alone in a dusty cave or barn when Jesus was born. Somehow, they found swaddling cloths to wrap him in. They placed him in a manger, a feeding tough for animals, when he went to sleep. I know this because I have seen it in manger scenes all across the country.

But what if it didn't happen exactly that way? I watched a Discovery Channel show a while back that said homes in those days were two story affairs where families lived on the upper level with animals on the lower level. "No room in the inn" might have meant no room was available in the living quarters. Mary and Joseph and the baby might have stayed downstairs. And there might well have been lots of family around to do the care giving. After all, Joseph did go to his family's community for the census, didn't he?

So, I wonder.

What if Jesus was not born in a lonely stable but in a loving home? What if, after his birth, he was passed from one family member to another until everyone had a chance to hold him? What if the

95

shepherds had to knock on the door to get in? I know it messes up thousands of years of manger scenes, but think about it.

What if Jesus really was one of us?

What if he cried when he was hungry and when the swaddling cloths were wrapped too tight? What if a bevy of Joseph's relatives took care of Mary until she was well again? What if Jesus didn't sleep through the night for six weeks or more and Mary got very tired of those two o'clock feedings? What if he didn't walk until he was a year old?

What if Jesus really was one of us?

And, as he grew, what if he played the same games other children played? What if he fought with his younger brothers and sisters from time to time, and what if first century time-outs were part of his life? What if Mary and Joseph made sure he got a good education and also made sure he knew the law and the prophets, which we call the Old Testament, backwards and forwards? What if he pestered his mother with questions, or begged his father to play with him when Joseph came home at night?

What if Jesus really was one of us?

Then, as an adult, what if Jesus had to struggle with his career choice? What if he had to decide between being a successful tradesman or a wandering rabbi? What if he loved going to wedding receptions and hanging out with friends? What if teaching was his passion and he used tried and true rabbinic storytelling methods to get his point across? What if he even fell in love? What if he felt the same pain of rejection we all feel when people denounced him, marginalized him, and condemned him?

What if Jesus really was one of us?

What if Jesus really was one of us and, at the same time, something more than us?

What if he was so tuned in to God that he called

God "Abba," which means "Daddy?" What if he was so immersed in scripture and prayer that he could accurately speak the Word of God to those who would listen? What if words like "commitment" and "faithfulness" meant something special to him? What if he was able to remain true to himself and his Abba, no matter what? And what if he was able to remain true all the way to the cross?

What if Jesus really was one of us and, at the same time, much more? What if he also was, as John's gospel says, a light that shines in the darkness?[1] And what if his way leads to the truth and the life?

What if...?

[1]John 1:5

How does this story challenge your image of Jesus?
Of his birth? Of his life?

Son of God

It happened this way.

He was born, they said, of a virgin mother who was impregnated by a god. He was adopted by his earthly father. As an adult, he established a kingdom of peace. He came to be called "Son of God," "Lord," "Redeemer," "Savior," and "Prince of Peace."

If you think this story is about Jesus of Nazareth, you are wrong.

This story is about Caesar Augustus, emperor of Rome.

He was born with the name Octavian. His uncle was Julius Caesar. After Julius Caesar was assassinated in 44 BC, the Roman Empire was wracked by a devastating civil war. The war ended when Octavian defeated Marc Antony and Cleopatra in battle in 31 BC. Octavian then ruled as Caesar Augustus until his death in 14 AD.

Caesar Augustus was an excellent leader, perhaps the kind we would all like to have. For one thing, he was a man with great integrity. He also gave people what they wanted most: peace and prosperity. Because he was so popular, he came to be called "Son Of God." Augustus helped this image along by having words like "divine" placed alongside his name on Roman coins.

So it was that, by the time of Jesus, if you used words like "Son of God" or "Prince of Peace," everyone knew you were talking about the emperor.

So now there comes on the scene this nomadic craftsman and rabbi. He is wildly popular with society's outcasts and just as wildly unpopular with much of society's elite. He is so popular with society's outsiders that they begin to call him "Messiah" and

"Son of God." This automatically raises the antennae of any Roman authority. Their job, after all, is to keep the peace at any price. He is accused of treason, or some such thing, and executed – which is what happens with revolutionaries. His followers don't give up on him, however, and continue to give him titles that, by rights, belong to Caesar.

What all that gives us today is a very interesting comparison between the way things are in the kingdoms of Caesar and the way scripture says things are in the kingdom of God.

In the kingdoms of Caesar, the general rule is "Win first, then bring peace." You capture a country, as Octavian did, and you put it back on its feet and rebuild its infrastructure. As long as it does what you want it to do, you support it.

In the kingdom of God, it is justice first, then peace. Justice comes through peacemaking, not violence. Justice comes by paying attention to the poor and the outsiders. It is following the way of Jesus, who was assertive without being violent.

In the kingdoms of Caesar, it is prosperity that counts. However, prosperity by definition always means prosperity for some and not for others. In Jesus' world, there was a huge gap between the "have's" and the "have-not's." The "have's" collected taxes from the "have-not's" in order to maintain their life styles. The "have-not's" lived in perpetual powerlessness and poverty.

In the kingdom of God, it is self-sacrifice that counts. Jesus said it again and again:

If you want to lead, be a servant.[1]

If you want to be successful, pick up your cross.[2]

If you want to be rich, store up treasures in heaven instead of buying more stuff.[3]

Specifically, he said:

Those who want to save their life will lose it, and those who lose their life for my sake and the sake of the gospel will find it.[4]

In the kingdoms of Caesar, approval is self-promoted. People were illiterate in the days of Caesar Augustus. One way of telling folks what was happening was to place images on coins that told stories. Caesar Augustus had special coins minted. His face was on one side of the coins, along with inscriptions like "The Divine Augustus." The other side of the coin showed pictures describing his triumphs.

In the kingdom of God, approval is found in faithfulness even if it means no public recognition. In one of Jesus' parables the righteous cried out, "Lord, when did we see you?" The answer came, "Whenever you did it to one of the least of these, you did it to me."[5] Faithfulness trumped recognition every time.

The challenge laid down in Jesus' day is still a challenge today. Who is the real Son of God? Is it the world's Caesars and the kingdoms as we understand them? Is it Jesus and the kind of kingdom he promoted? Which kingdom do we choose to live in? After all, the kingdoms of the Caesars sound awfully appealing, especially if you are on the winning side.

Perhaps one clue to the answer is this:

Very few people know these days who Caesar Augustus was. He lived and died, and so did his empire. Each Sunday morning, millions of people around the world gather to sing that Jesus Christ is Lord.

[1]Mark 10:43-44
[2]Mark 8:343-36
[3]Matthew 6:19-21
[4]Mark 8:35
[5]Matthew 25:40

Reflect:

Would you like to have a Caesar Augustus be your country's leader? Why, or why not?

What, to you, is the difference between the kingdoms of your world and the kingdom of God?

Herod

(Luke 3:1-14; Mark 6:14-29)

I am Herod Antipas, tetrarch of Galilee and Perea, and son of Herod the Great. I am in charge and I will be in charge and no one had better get in my way. My legacy will be one of peace, no matter what I have to do to get it. Future generations will hail me as the one who rebuilt Sepphoris after the revolt, and of building the beautiful seaside city of Tiberias, named after our glorious emperor. Nothing will tarnish my image. Nothing!

People call me brutal. So what? They have no power. My reach extends from the shores of the great sea clear down South to the Judean wilderness. I hear things. I know when trouble is brewing, and I handle it. Take, for example, this baptizer down by the Dead Sea.

His name was John. He came out of nowhere and started preaching repentance. Told everyone to change their ways, or else. Turn to the one God, he shouted. Then he took an old bathing ritual and used it for something different. He immersed people in the Jordan River as a sign of their changed life. He was a crazy looking character with a strange diet. Mostly, I thought he was a crackpot, just like so many others. Sure, he attracted people. In fact, men and women walked for days just to hear him. But I figured he was harmless as long as he stuck to preaching and baptizing.

Then he started meddling in my life. He called me out for marrying Herodias. I suppose I have to tell you that story so you'll understand. I was married to Phasaelis, daughter of the king of Nabatea. So far, so good. Then, when I was staying in Rome with my half-brother (who was also named Herod, Herod Philip), I fell in love with his wife Herodias. I divorced Phasaelis and married Herodias. This made the king of Nabatea mad, and it didn't endear me to my brother. So what? I got what I wanted, just as I always do.

The baptizer condemned me and condemned my marriage. He said I went against Jewish law. Sure, I am a Jew. I go to Jerusalem for the high holy days. Again, so what? I am the one in charge, and he cannot say things like that. Besides, he might stir up the crowd and they are nervous enough as it is. I did what I had to do. I arrested him and threw him in prison. I thought I would be done with him.

Herodias wasn't happy with him either. In fact, she wanted him dead. She got her wish.

Last night, I held a party. We had great food and lots to drink. We had a very good time! In the middle of the party, Herodias' daughter came and danced for us. It was everything I could ask for. She was beautiful and graceful, and she showed my guests how great I really am. When she finished, I offered her anything she wanted. After all, people need to know I am a generous man when I want to be. She consulted with her mother, and then asked for the baptizer's head on a platter.

What could I do? I gave her what she asked for. Besides, that's one more troublemaker out of the way. Now I can go back to doing what I do best.

Lately, though, I have been hearing some strange rumblings. I have been told a relative of the baptizer is starting to attract a following. He comes from Nazareth, they say. Nazareth, of all places! He teaches like no one else, I am told. and even heals people. He also talks about a new kingdom. I can't have that. There can only be one kingdom, and that is mine! I will watch him very carefully. Perhaps, one day, I will deal with him as well.

After all, I am Herod Antipas, tetrarch of Galilee and Perea, and son of Herod the Great.

Reflect:

What do your leaders typically do when their power is threatened?

What do you typically do when your authority is questioned?

How do you compare Herod's authority with that of Jesus?

The Invitation

(Mark 1:16-20)

It is early morning. Waves from the Sea of Galilee caress the rocky shoreline. The sun has risen over the hills to the East, and it looks to be another hot day. Boats are being pulled up on shore after a long night of fishing. The pulling and heaving is accompanied by the customary cursing and grumbling. Fish are transferred from boat to carts for transport to the market. Gulls dance in the air; squawking, diving, and fighting for any particle of food that drops to the ground. Fishermen set about the task of drying their nets, patching any holes in the webbing, and preparing them for the next night's fishing. They are tired and hungry, but this one last job must be done.

Two sets of brothers are among the fishermen. They are Simon and Andrew, son of Jonah, and James and John, son of Zebedee. Simon is the most impetuous of them all. He is well known for making quick decisions and speaking out of turn. He is the extrovert of the bunch. Everyone knows when Simon is around. Andrew is the quieter of the two brothers, and yet he is well respected. He lives in nearby Capernaum, as does his brother. People call James and John the sons of thunder. They come from an affluent family, as is evidenced by the hired men working in Zebedee's boat. They do like to argue with one another. They too live in Capernaum.

On this particular morning, the rabbi Jesus walks along the shore and steps over to the boat where Simon and Andrew are working. They already know him, for he has made his home in their community. Perhaps they have worshipped together at the synagogue services. Perhaps they have even spent time with him, listening to him and getting to know him. Perhaps they are even impressed by his message about living in an alternative kingdom to the one mandated by the oppressive Roman and Jewish rulers.

The three men talk for a bit, and then Jesus offers a strange invitation. "Come with me," he says. "I will teach you a new kind of fishing." This presents the brothers with a challenge. Their livelihood is here on the water. The nets are not completely dry. How will Simon support his wife and family and mother-in-law? Neither Simon nor Andrew ever traveled more than 20 miles from home. This is the only world they know. What is Jesus asking of them? And yet…

For reasons no one will ever explain, they drop everything. They drop everything they know and everything they own. And they follow him.

A few minutes later, the trio meets James and John. They too are cleaning up the boat and getting ready to go home. They are with their father and the hired hands. James, John, and even Zebedee recognize their guest. Out of hospitality, they offer something to drink and a slice of bread from home. Once again, they talk. Then Jesus offers James and John the same invitation. Not Zebedee; not the hired hands; only James and John. Once again, the challenge is presented. If they leave, their father will have no one to pass his business along to. If they leave, they face a very uncertain financial future. And what does their father have to say about all this? One can only imagine the catch in his throat and the thunder in his voice as he responds. And yet…

James and John too drop everything. They drop everything they know and follow Jesus into the unknown.

Little do they know that they will spend the next two years with this unusual man. Little do they know that they will travel to places where no right-thinking Jew would ever dream of going. Little do they know they will face danger, hostility, and will even have to leave their homeland from time to time for their own safety. Little do they know that they will be part of an inner circle of learners, or that Jesus will attract a wide following as he teaches and heals across the countryside. Little do they know that they will witness a violent execution, or a life-changing surprise. Little do they know that James will become a leader in a fledgling band of believers who will be called "the Way," or that Peter will play a leading role in the faith community, or that they will face martyrdom.

Little do they know. They simply make a decision. They drop what they are doing. They follow.

Reflect:

What would you have done if you were one of these brothers?

How do you typically make life changing decisions?

What does this story say to you?

Furious

(Luke 4:14-30)

Hello Benjamin, my friend. Welcome to my home! May I get you something to drink? Some fresh baked bread to eat, perhaps? You weren't here yesterday, were you? I heard you were visiting relatives in Cana. You didn't hear what happened? Let me tell you. It was terrible! I was furious! More than furious! Words escape me to tell you how I felt.

You know we are a small village. With only 60 families, everyone knows everyone else. Yes, everyone knows everyone else's business too, but that's beside the point. You know Jesus? Of course you do, Mary and Joseph's son. He grew up here. He played with my children and learned a trade from his father. You know all that.

You know too that he has been away. Someone said he was down south at Qumran, learning from the Essenes. Who knows? Maybe that's just a rumor. Someone else said he met up with his cousin John and spent time with him. We all know he has been back in Galilee for some time, going from village to village. He has been gaining a reputation as a teacher and healer. Of course, you know that too. Well, this week he came home. Yesterday, on the Sabbath, he came to our synagogue service.

You know we are too small to have a special place for worship, so we gather in our town building. As long as we have a minion of 10 men we can meet. That is what we did yesterday. We did the things we always do on the Sabbath. We recited the Shema: "Hear, O Israel, the Lord our God, the Lord is one."[1] We stood for the Eighteen Benedictions, our prayers thanking God for all that has been done for us in our past and honoring God's holiness.

Then someone handed Jesus the scroll with the reading for the day and he stood to read it to us. As you know, someone always stands for the reading of the ancient texts. This time, the scroll was opened to the prophet Isaiah. I still remember the words, because... Well, you'll see.

The reading went something like this:
    The Spirit of the Lord is upon me,
    Because he has anointed me
    To bring good news to the poor,
    To proclaim release to the captives,
    And recovery of sight to the blind.[2]

Then Jesus gave the scroll back and, as is our custom, he sat down to teach. We couldn't wait to hear what he said next. After all, he is one of us, and we have heard great things from other places he has been. He looked up at us and said, "This reading just came true, right in front of your eyes."

Well, everybody started talking at once.
    Someone said, "Yes, this is what we wanted to hear."
    Someone else inquired, "Isn't he Joseph's son?"
    Still another exclaimed, "What a brilliant young man."
    A fourth person cried out, "Isn't it wonderful that he came home to be with us today?"

I wish he had stopped right there. I wish he had just kept his mouth shut! But oh no! He did not! He looked straight in our eyes and said prophets are respected everywhere except in their home town. He also said he supposed we wanted him to do the same things for us that he did in Capernaum. Well, of course we did. What's the matter with that? After all, he grew up here. Don't we deserve some favors? We weren't thinking such kind thoughts after that. Even then he wasn't finished.

He said there were lots of hungry widows in our country during the famine that took place in Elijah's time, but Elijah was sent to a widow in Sidon, over in gentile country. Then he said many lepers lived in our country when Elisha was alive, but Elisha didn't cleanse any one of them. Instead, he healed Naaman the Syrian, who was by no means one of us.

We knew right away what he was trying to tell us. Our little world is too small, he was saying. Why should we expect any special favors, he was saying. The poor, the captives, and the blind he was sent to recover and release include people we don't want any part of, he was saying.

Well, that's no way to talk! Haven't we suffered? Haven't we kept the faith? Haven't we obeyed the law? Haven't we kept our synagogue alive? Don't we deserve a little good news from time to time? Why waste so much effort on those people?

We were incensed! I was incensed! We hauled this so-called favorite son of ours out of town and dragged him to the crest of the steep hill. You know where it is. We were ready to toss him down that hill and hope that he rolled all the way to the bottom. I don't know why we didn't. The good news is that he left, and I say good riddance!

Now, my friend, enough of that. What is past is past. We won't have to deal with him again. Life can continue as we know it. Now, tell me. How is it with you? Let's just sit and talk a while, shall we?

[1]Deuteronomy 6:4
[2]Isaiah 61:1-3

Reflect:

What would you have been thinking if you were a part of that synagogue service?

What would you have done?

How does your understanding of Jesus challenge your presumptions?

Where are you challenged by Christ to move out of your comfort zone?

What are you doing about it?

Our Father[1]

A One Act Play
(Matthew 6:7-15)

A man walks hesitantly into an empty church sanctuary and looks around. He wears jeans, a golf shirt, and sneakers.

Man: Hello? Is anybody there? The door was open, so I came in. I don't know why. (He walks around and stands in front of the cross.) I haven't prayed or anything for a long time. I suppose I should, since I am in here and all. Let's see. Where should I start? Oh yes. I learned this a long time ago. (He clears his throat.) Our Father, who art in heaven…

Voice: Yes?

Man: (Startled) Who's there?

Voice: God. You asked for me.

Man: No I didn't. I mean, I was just saying… Jack, is that you? Quit fooling around!

Voice: I am not fooling. Get on with it.

Man: Come on. Quit joking around. I'm serious.

Voice: So am I. Now say what you were going to say.

Man: Our father, who art in heaven…

Voice: I am not just in heaven, you know.

Man: (Exasperated) Where are you then? I can't see you.

Voice: I am like the wind. You can't see the wind either, but you know it's there. I am there too.

Man: Right. (Resumes) Our Father, who art in heaven, hallowed be thy name.

115

Voice: Thank you.

Man: For what?

Voice: For recognizing that my name is special.

Man: Can I please continue? I have a lunch date.

Voice: Keep going.

Man: Thy kingdom come, thy will be done on earth as it is in heaven.

Voice: Do you mean it?

Man: Mean what?

Voice: Do you really want my will to be done?

Man: Of course. At least, I think so? What are you getting at?

Voice: If you want my will to be done, a lot of things will need to change. In fact, you will need to make some changes.

Man: Yeah, well. I was just saying it anyway.

Voice: Maybe you need to watch what you say.

Man: Jack, are you hiding somewhere? Will you cut that out!

Voice: I am NOT Jack. Now, keep going.

Man: Give us this day our daily bread.

Voice: I already gave you everything you need, but you said it wasn't enough.

Man: You're messing with my head again.

Voice: When you said us, you really meant you, didn't you? Are you interested in the daily bread of the homeless family you passed on your way in here? What do you mean by what you just said?

Man: I guess I meant... Hey! It's just a prayer.

Voice: If you say so.

Man: Forgive us – I mean, me – our, uh my, trespasses as I forgive those who trespass against me.

Voice: Are you asking me to forgive you in the same way you forgive the people you have a grudge against?

Man: (Frustrated) I don't know. Do you mean I am really supposed to let go of this thing I have against my brother-in-law? Or my boss?

Voice: What do you think?

Man: And that you are willing to forgive me to the extent that I am willing to forgive others?

Voice: Think about it.

Man: I may need a little more forgiveness than that. (Silence) Can I go on now?

Voice: Be my guest.

Man: And lead me not into temptation, but deliver me from evil.

Voice: I'll try.

Man: What do you mean, you'll try?

Voice: You need to help me out a little here. I'll guide you, but you need to do your part too; like flirting with that brunette at the office. You need to pay attention to the boundaries I set up for you.

Man: How did you know about that? Forget what I just said.

Voice: Anything else?

Man: (Speaking quickly) For thine is the kingdom and the power and the glory forever.

Voice: Yes it is. And don't forget it. Do you have anything else to say?

Man: Amen?

Voice: Yes. Let it be so.

Man: (Preparing to leave) Um. Can I come back again sometime?

Voice: Any time at all. I will be here, or there, or wherever you are. By the way, thank you for coming.

Man: You're.. You're welcome. (Exits)

Reflect:

What is the most powerful part of the Lord's Prayer for you?
What is the most challenging?

[1]Others have written plays based on the Lord's Prayer. This is my version.
If you were writing this script, what would you say?

Barefoot in a Pig Sty[1]

(Luke 15:11-32)

The Younger Son:
I am the *younger* of two sons, and I was tired of it all. I was tired of working in my father's business; tired of being the youngest; tired of hanging around the house and doing the same things day after day. Life had to be more fun almost anywhere else.

So, I did the unthinkable. I asked for my share of the inheritance. By law, it was only half of what my older brother gets. After all, the oldest son has all the rights. But I suppose something is better than nothing. I knew I was humiliating my family. You just don't do things like that. And, because my family lives in a close-knit community, I was humiliating the whole town as well.

I didn't care. I took the money and ran.

I left the country and went to the city, with all it had to offer. When I walked around those streets, I was bug-eyed and jaw-dropped for days! I went to the theaters; I saw the plays. Their values were different from the ones I learned while growing up, but who cares? I went to the chariot races, and watched as people and animals were killed. I knew Jewish law requires kindness, but this was a *lot* more exciting. All over the city, I saw the naked images and the statues to the gods. They didn't teach me this stuff down on the farm!

I spent my inheritance like there was no tomorrow. When that was gone, I borrowed money from friends. Then I borrowed some more. Then...

Then the money dried up. My "friends" disappeared. Creditors started calling. I couldn't pay. I suffered the debtor's fate. I was thrown into prison.

Eventually, a Gentile farmer paid my debt. I became his servant. This meant I had to work for him for seven years before my debt could be forgiven. At first, I was just glad to be out of jail. Then things went from bad to worse.

I had to work with pigs. The farmer didn't feed me well, and I got so hungry that I actually ate the slop the pigs ate. I was raised to be a good Jew, even though you wouldn't know it by what I was doing. By law, Jews don't eat pork. They don't even associate with pigs. To feed these awful animals and to eat the food they ate... Well, I hit bottom. Has that ever happened to you? Have you ever hit bottom physically, emotionally, or spiritually?

I decided to go back home. I knew my inheritance was gone for good, so I planned to beg my father to let me be his servant. It would be better to be a servant in my father's house than to be barefoot in a pig sty!

I didn't expect much. After all, I had humiliated everyone. If worse came to worst, the town would run me out and stone me. Even so, I went home.

All the way home, I rehearsed my three-point argument: I have sinned. I am no longer worthy. Make me your servant. I repeated it over and over again. I hoped I had it right.

I knew I was out of control, I just didn't know how much. Until my father saw me. My father did the unthinkable! He *ran* to me. Grown men don't run! He didn't care if the whole village saw him. He *ran* to me, and he *hugged* me, and he *kissed* me.

I started my speech, but he never let me get to the servant part. Instead, he started shouting orders. Each order had the power of a sledge hammer of grace.

"Bring him the robe! Not that one! My prayer shawl!" I was welcomed back into the family.

"Put a ring on his finger!" It was the family signet ring, the family credit card. I was restored to wealth.

120

"Put sandals on his feet!" The only people who go barefoot are slaves and servants. My father was saying, "You are no slave; you are my son!"

"Throw a party!" To throw a party for someone means you are bound together in friendship for life.

I was home again. I was home, and I belonged.

The Older Son:

I am the *oldest* brother. I am the *responsible* brother. I am the *respectable* brother. I have rights of inheritance. Look it up. It's in the law.

I have worked hard to protect my father's investments. I was always there for him. I got my hands dirty. I took care of the family business. I did what I was expected to do; what I was supposed to do. I played by the rules. Meanwhile, my little brother decided the grass was greener in the city. He took his share of the inheritance and left home. He disgraced all of us!

Tonight I came home to the sounds of a party. When I asked around, I found out little brother is home again. I also found out my father restored him to full membership in the family. Even gave him financial rights.

I am *furious*!

I am *not* going into that house. That money, or what is left of it, is mine! The very least my father could have done was consult with me first. I would have told him what little brother could do with his tale of woe. But, oh no; father gives him a full pardon and a warm welcome home. No, I am not going to join that party!

Now, I see Father coming to me. It's an insult, making him come to me instead of me going to him, but I don't care. He tries to talk to me, but I don't listen. I shout back.

"I worked hard for you! I stayed here! I did what I was supposed to do! He… He ran out! Now you're throwing a party for him? What have you ever, ever done for me?"

It's not fair, I suppose. All my father ever did was to give me the keys to the family business and make sure I had personal comfort and prestige and the challenge of a successful career. But I am angry.

I don't want to remember!

> *We who are part of a church gather from time to time at the Lord's table. We don't come because we've earned it or because there is some clause in our contract that says we deserve it. We come because we know, deep down, this story is about us. Some of us have run away and then returned. Some of us are stay-at-home prodigals who have also run away from the arms of grace. Some of us have even done both. We come, not because we deserve it, but because we are invited. We come, and the Christ of eternity offers us – not a robe or a ring or sandals – but a simple slice of bread and an ordinary cup of juice. And, in that offering, says, "Welcome home! Everything I have is yours. Come with me; join the party. I've set a place for you at the table."*

[1]This phrase came from Jim Fleming's book, *The Parables of Jesus*. Biblical Resources. PO Box 3900. LaGrange, Georgia, 30241. Copyright 2001.

Reflect:

When have you been the youngest son?
The oldest? The father?

Where in your life do you need to be welcomed home?

Where do you need to say "Welcome home!"
to someone else?

The Jericho Road

(Luke 10:25-37)

The Jericho Road runs for about 22 miles between Jerusalem and Jericho. If you are on your way to Jericho, you are going downhill because that's the only thing you can do. The elevation drops more then 3,600 feet, making Jericho the lowest community on the face of the earth. The Jericho Road winds around hills and rocks through a rugged mountainous terrain called the Judean Desert. During the time when Jesus told this story, thieves hid in the turns and crevasses, attacking unsuspecting travelers. No one in their right mind walked that road alone!

Jesus said simply, "A man was going down from Jerusalem to Jericho." Right away, his listeners knew the man did something incredibly stupid. He was asking for trouble, and he got it. Thieves attacked the man, robbed him, and left him for dead. What else would you expect, his listeners wondered. It is like people who pass you in the fast lane when the road is icy. When you see them in the ditch a mile ahead, you think they got what they deserved. So it was with this man. So it was with Jesus' listeners.

Would you take time to help someone who got in trouble from doing something really stupid? Would you expect someone to help you out of a self-imposed crisis?

You wouldn't expect many people to travel that rugged road every day but, in Jesus' story, a couple of people did. They were a priest and a rabbi. These were people to be looked up to. They knew the law. They knew what needed to be done. They had the answers. And the answer was this:

If you have done the hard, time-consuming work to make yourself ritually pure, and if you touch anything bloody, you have to endure days of ritual cleansing all over again. It is best not to get into that predicament.

They knew the right answer, so they stepped over to the other side of the road to avoid getting soiled. They just kept going.

But, on the other hand, these men were going *down* the road. This meant they weren't going uphill to the sacred Temple in Jerusalem. They had already performed the duties that required ritual purity. Maybe they didn't need to be pure any more. Maybe they just didn't want to get involved.

Ever since this story was first told, these two men have been cast as the bad guys. They knew the law, but they forgot the overarching principle about loving a neighbor. The nagging question is, how often do we do the same? When do we pass by on the other side?

Finally, along came the good guy. Only, he was not really a good guy. Remember, Jesus' listeners were Jews. This guy was a Samaritan. Jews hated Samaritans, and had hated them for hundreds of years. For Jews, Samaritans were the scum of the earth. You can imagine the internal squirming that took place when Jesus took this scum and transformed him into a hero. The Samaritan did the right thing. He did the messy thing. He helped the man, who by rights deserved no help.

Have you ever played the Samaritan's role? Have you ever stopped to help, even though you were an outsider? Or, have you ever accepted help from one of the Samaritans of your world? Where have you

126

seen the right thing done; the messy thing done?

Somehow, the Samaritan transported the beaten man to Jericho. In that oasis town, he found an innkeeper who took that man in and cared for him until he was on his feet again. Innkeepers don't show up much in the stories around Jesus. We know there was no room in the inn when Jesus was born. And we know this innkeeper took care of this man in Jesus' story. What happened here is what happens a hundred times a day. The innkeeper did good by doing his job.

When have you done the right thing just by doing your job? When has someone treated you well simply in the performance of duty?

The punch line:
Jesus paused at the end of the story and asked, "Who was the real neighbor?" His Jewish listener swallowed hard, and gave the only answer that was possible to give.

This story started when a lawyer asked what it was like to live in God's kingdom. Jesus said, it means getting your hands dirty. It means doing what needs to be done. It means being a neighbor, even to a stranger. Even to an enemy.

Whenever you begin to wonder who your neighbor is, remember Jesus' story. Once upon a time, a man was going down the road from Jerusalem to Jericho.

Reflect:

Consider the questions embedded in this story.
What do your answers say to you?

I See

(John 9)

Y-yes sirs. I do know who you are. You are the Pharisees. It is your job to make certain we keep the faith in these troubled times. Yes sir. I know that. I have never talked to a Pharisee before. I know you are powerful, and I am kind of nervous.

Do I know why you called me here? I... I think so. You want to know what happened.

Do you know I was blind from birth? You do. You have been checking up on me. You believe I was blind because I sinned, or else my parents sinned. Everybody thinks that. I have carried that burden since I was very young. I could not see, and I was blamed for it. No sir. I am not criticizing you. I am just telling you what it has been like.

Yes, get on with it. Of course.

I was sitting by the roadside begging for money, as always, when some people walked by. One of the men saw me and asked a rabbi who it was that sinned and caused me to be born blind. Was it my parents, or me? Like I said, I get that a lot. The rabbi answered that no one sinned. Then the rabbi came over to me. I do not get that a lot. I heard him spit on the ground. Then I think he did something with the dirt. The next thing I knew, he covered my eyes with this muddy stuff and told me to go to the pool of Siloam and wash myself off in the healing waters. Of course, someone had to lead me there, just like always.

When I left the pool, I could see for the first time in my life! You don't believe me? Neither did my neighbors. At first they argued about me. Some said I was the same person who sat and begged all day long. Others argued that I just looked like that man. I had to convince them that I am the same man they saw by the roadside this morning. Then they asked how it was that I could see. I told them about this man. His name was Jesus, by the way. They asked me where he was, and I said I did not know.

When did this happen? Well, just today. You know, the Sabbath day. What? He worked on the Sabbath because he made mud, so he cannot be from God? Well, you certainly know more about the law than I do. What do I think? I think he is a prophet.

You still don't believe me? You asked my parents if I was their son? What did they say? They told you I am their son and that I was born blind, but they don't know how I received my sight? And they told you I can speak for myself? Well, I don't mean to show disrespect, but that is what I am trying to do.

You want me to tell the truth? You want me to say this Jesus is a sinner? Let me answer this way. I do not know if he is a sinner or not. All I know is that I was blind, but now I can see.

Sir? You want me to tell my story all over again? Why? You didn't listen to me before. Do you want to become his follower or something? You tell me you just want to know where he comes from. You know what I think? I do not believe I am a sinner, as you keep insisting, and I do not believe he is a sinner either. I think he comes from God.

What? You are excommunicating me? Throwing me out of the synagogue? I can see again and you, sir, apparently can not. Thank you for your time.

Reflect:

What do you typically do when your beliefs are challenged?

What is the symbolism of seeing and not seeing in this story?

What does this story say to you?

The Storm

(Mark 4:35-41)

You are the Jesus-follower history forgot. Everyone knows Peter. Almost everyone knows James and John; and, of course, Judas. But not you. Your name is listed among the 12, but who you are and what you did is lost to history, only to be resurrected through traditions that gather like moss around an old tree. On this day, however, none of that is important.

You have been with Jesus down by the Galilean sea all day. You listened to him tell a funny story about a mustard seed. (Mustard is a weed, for heaven's sake. How can the kingdom be like mustard?) You heard another story about a sower's battle to raise a crop, and you wondered what it meant. (Everyone knows farmers have a tough time of it. What was Jesus trying to say?)

Now, evening has come. It is time to relax, perhaps have a little something to eat, and rest. Tomorrow will likely be another busy day. Instead, Jesus says, "Let's get in a boat and go to the other side." You can immediately think of several reasons why this is a bad idea. For one thing, it is almost dark. You don't relish the idea of being on the water in the middle of the night. Second, you know what he means by "the other side" and you don't want to go there. The "other side" is where the gentiles live. They aren't Jews, and good people like you try to avoid them at all costs.

Third, you are frankly afraid of the water. You are not a fisherman like some of the others. Your roots are among the desert people, and you learned from childhood that the seas are a dangerous place. Chaos is in the water; and death. Horrible things happen when people confront the raging deep. You would rather do almost anything than get in that boat at sunset and take a several hour sail to "the other side."

Yet, you go.

A gentle breeze from the east is in your face as you push off from shore. The sailors among you tack the boat to the south and then to the north, angling it into the wind. The wind and the slapping of the waves against the hull calm even your shaky nerves. Talk about the day's events drifts into a drowsy silence. After an hour or so, Jesus falls asleep in the stern, resting against a cushion.

You do not know it – how could you? – but the sea is a trickster. The eastern shore line on "the other side" features high bluffs scarred by deep canyons that run down into the water. The winds on the bluffs pick up speed as they blow down through the canyons until, from time to time, they hammer the water with hurricane force. A calm sea transforms into a raging maelstrom in a matter of minutes.

You are jolted out of your reverie by a sudden pounding of water against the hull. The rigging starts to whistle from the wind, and the boat rapidly picks up speed. Some of the men trim the sails; worried looks fill the faces of even the hardened seafarers. You are terrified. This is what you feared most.

It gets worse. Sea water splashes over the side and slops on your feet. Those of you who aren't trying to manage the boat begin to bail water with anything you can get your hands on. It's a losing battle. More water fills the boat with each wave. Someone shrieks that you are about to capsize. Your worst nightmare calls your name. The chaos... The death… The horror… You panic.

Jesus, meanwhile, still sleeps. Some of you prod him, shout to him, and wake him up. Terrified, you cry at him. "We're drowning! Don't you care? Help us!"

Then, the impossible becomes possible. Jesus gets up, shakes off his sleep, stares into the teeth of the storm, and shouts "Peace! Be still!" Just that quickly, the wind dies away. The sea flattens out. The storm is over. Jesus shrugs and turns to those of you who stare slack jawed at him. "What are you afraid of?" he asks. You don't know what to say. Who is this man, you wonder, who takes my worst nightmare and makes it go away?

134

After a time, the breeze picks up again and you continue your journey to "the other side."

Reflect:

When in your life have you been drifting with the breeze?

When have you been caught up in a raging emotional storm?

What terrifies you?

Where do you need to hear the words, "Peace! Be still?"

When have you heard those words in the past?

What does this story say to you right now?

Resort Town

(Matthew 16:13-23; Mark 8:27-38; Luke 9:18-23)

Perhaps he and his students are in the region of Caesarea Philippi on vacation. After all, these headwaters of the Jordan River are a popular spot for folks who want to escape the heat. Here in the mountains north of Galilee, the river dances over rocks as children splash in the shallows. Perhaps they are here on vacation.

Or perhaps they are here for a more serious reason. Perhaps they need to be somewhere safe.

Some years ago, Herod the Great ruled over this whole region. This was the Herod of Jesus' birth, the Herod who was ruthless and violent and held on to power at all costs. The Jews secretly called him Herod the Monstrous. When he died, some say from tapeworm, his territory was divided among his three sons Herod, Herod, and Herod. Herod Antipas now rules the area that includes Galilee, where Jesus conducts most of his ministry. This Herod is just as brutal as his father was. This Herod beheaded John the Baptist because he was entranced by a dancing girl. And this Herod has asked to "see" Jesus, possibly in the way he once wanted to "see" John the Baptist.

Herod Philip is more tolerant, mostly because he can't stand his brother Herod Antipas. A woman is involved in that feud, but that is a different story. Herod Philip rules the area that includes Caesarea, and he allows Jesus to roam there in freedom. The third Herod didn't last long, and is not a part of this tale.

Perhaps Jesus is in Caesarea because he needed to be somewhere safe.

One day, he asks his students, "Who do people say I am? What are people saying about me?" It is like giving a pop quiz where those who know the answer raise their hands right away. "Well," one of them answers, "some folks are saying you are John the Baptist come back to life." "Yes," another says, "and others think you are Elijah or one of the prophets." That makes sense. Lots of people those days expect their rescuer to be an Elijah.

He thinks about that for a while. Then he asks, "Well, what do you think? Who do you think I am?" Like students given a tough question, you can imagine hands disappearing from sight. Dead silence. Simon is the one with the gift for speaking before thinking and often putting his foot in his mouth. He blurts out, "You are the Messiah!"

"That's great Simon," He answers. He points to a massive rock face nearby. They can't miss it. The stream flowing out of that rock is an important source of water for the Jordan River. He says, "I'm going to call you 'Rock,' and on this rock of what you said a new world is being formed."

They listen intently as they try to sort out what he just said. Then he starts to talk about going to Jerusalem and being killed. Rock takes him aside and tells him he is dead wrong. This isn't part of the "Messiah Master Plan." But the answer comes back. "Get out of my sight! You're just not getting it!" Then the great man calls his students together, along with some other folks who are listening in. "What I am talking about is dangerous stuff," he tells them. "If you want to follow me, you'd better be ready to let go of anything that holds you back and pick up a cross."

After that, they leave Caesarea Philippi and head back toward the territory governed by the other Herod. The students don't know it yet, but they are about to learn a hard lesson as they travel along the Jordan and up the hill to Jerusalem and beyond.

The students sometimes "got it," and sometimes they did not. Some things don't change. So it was, and so it is.

Reflect:

Who do you say Jesus is?

As you think about living in the way of Jesus,
when do you "get it?"

When do you not "get it?"

A Centurion's Report

(Mark 11:1-11)

Yes, Sir. Thank you for seeing me. I am here to report, as requested.

I am certain you realize that Jerusalem is crowded with tourists this time of year. People come from all over to celebrate the Passover, and the city more than doubles in size. We also get our share of crackpots who want to announce some crazy message or another, and we have to be especially careful that the city isn't infiltrated by terrorists who want to cut our throats. That is why we arrive early, and the 80 men in my command are trained to be on the lookout for any sign of trouble. As you know, Rome will not tolerate any form of rebellion or dissent.

This may seem off the subject, but please humor me for a moment. Every now and then, someone comes along who claims to be Israel's long-awaited Messiah. Some of them climb up to the highest point in the Temple and announce their message. Mostly, they are harmless and no one pays attention. Every now and again we have to step in and make sure these guys disappear, if you know what I mean. Remember Theudas or Judas of Galilee? They attracted hundreds of people, but we followed the old adage that the best way to get rid of a snake is to cut off its head. After they died, their followers disappeared.

That brings me to what happened today. We received word late this afternoon that trouble was brewing on the Mount of Olives. Some rabbi from the hill country was coming into town, and our spies reported he had picked up a crowd. I stationed my men along the city walls and doubled the guard at the gates. They were all armed, of course, with their spears and knives and crossbows. I told them not to initiate anything, but to be very alert. If this guy wanted to start trouble, we would be sure to finish it.

We saw them before we could hear them. The rabbi and his entourage were winding their way down to the Kidron Valley. When I first saw them, he was riding a donkey. I didn't understand what that was all about, but one of my soldiers told me it had something to do with Jewish prophecy. The word was that a new king will come into town riding on a donkey instead of in a royal procession. He will establish a new kingdom that will stretch from sea to sea and will order all nations to be at peace. That sounded to me like a direct attack on Rome, so when I heard this, I ordered my troops to form up for battle.

When they drew closer to the gate, I could see and hear what was going on. People were waving palm branches and singing one of their psalms. It went something like "Save us now!" and "Here comes the one God has blessed." I didn't catch all of it. As you know, the palm branches are a symbol of Jewish rebellion and a way of showing how much these people hate us. When they added their song to the waving of the palms, I was certain we were headed for a confrontation that would be violent and bloody. I was ready, and I was prepared to give the order to hit them hard.

What actually happened was exactly the opposite of what I expected. No one raised a sword. No one tried to attack us. No one even shouted at us in anger. This rabbi simply entered the city, went to the Temple, looked around for a few minutes, and left!

I ordered the troops to stand down and we ended up with a very routine day.

Sir, I recommend that we keep an eye on this rabbi. While he did nothing to cause us any harm, the warning signs were all there. Remember, I saw the palm branches waving and I heard the people shouting for someone to rescue them. I am suspicious that he may indeed be trying to install a new kingdom here in this corner of Rome's empire. Trouble may come in the days ahead.

Sir, may I ask, what do you make of all this? Based on my report, what are your orders?

Reflect:

Imagine you are one of the people not mentioned in the Palm Sunday stories.

Perhaps you are a member of the crowd or a soldier on the walls; or a Jewish leader trying to keep the faith in troubled times.

Read the story through the eyes of one of these people. How does it change your perception of what happened?

It's Over

(Mark 14-15)

It's over. It's finally, mercifully, over.

I went out to the road into town where they do the executions. The others are still there, still dying, but he is gone. Someone took his body down; they put him in a borrowed grave until they can have a proper burial.

I can't believe this has happened, and yet we all saw it coming. We knew Jerusalem would be dangerous this Passover season; and so did he. Herod Antipas would be here. Herod has been after him for a long time. Pilate would be here too. Roman soldiers would be out in force, looking for any sign of insurrection. It happened before; it might happen again. We begged him not to come. If he was so determined to be here, we hoped he would at least keep quiet about it.

He did just the opposite.

It started when he came into the city. He had us get him a donkey and take it out to Bethany. Then he mounted the donkey and rode it toward the walls of the city. Any Jew with a brain knew what he was doing. It fulfilled the prophecy that said the king would ride into Jerusalem on a donkey. Well, you know what happened next. A crowd gathered. Then they started waving palm branches. Palm branches, of all things. Even the Romans knew this was a sign of rebellion. The crowds shouted, "Save us! Save us now!" It couldn't get any worse! Fortunately, nothing happened. At least, not then. But the Romans were on guard.

It just didn't get any better after that. When he went to the Temple, he tossed out the people who were taking advantage of the poor by selling sacrificial animals at exorbitant prices. Then he argued with just about everyone in authority, and challenged their rigid belief systems. It was almost as if he was looking to get himself killed.

In the end, it wasn't the Romans who got him, and it wasn't the Jewish authorities. It was one of us. Our trusted friend, Judas, betrayed him. I don't know. Maybe Judas thought like the crowds did, that he would take over and drive out the Romans; or at least clean out the Temple hypocrisy. I guess we'll never know why. It happened just last night, after our Passover meal. We walked outside the city walls, across the valley, and climbed the hill. He went into a grove of olive trees to pray. That's where Judas led them. That's where they arrested him.

All night long, they interrogated him. They laughed at him. Other so-called messiahs came and went. If he was so special, they asked, why didn't he save himself? At least, that's what we heard they did. Then they bounced him back and forth between the Jewish leaders and the Roman leaders. Who would get the chance to execute him? If it was the Jewish leaders, they would stone him. The Romans had their own several forms of cruelty. Finally, the power of Rome took over. That's when they decided to crucify him, but not before they beat him nearly senseless and forced him to carry his own cross.

I couldn't watch. I just couldn't bear it. Some of the women stayed. They watched the whole thing. They were braver than we men were. Maybe they thought the authorities wouldn't arrest them. All I know is that I ran for my life. I have been sneaking around the city ever since.

I thought he was the answer. That's why I listened to him every chance I got. That's why I followed him here. I thought, finally, we would be saved from all this meanness and cruelty. It didn't happen.

It's over.

Reflect:

If you were there, what would you be thinking
and doing on the night Jesus was crucified?

What has the church taught you about Jesus' crucifixion?

What does Jesus' crucifixion mean to you?

Chuckle from Heaven

(Luke 24:1-12)

Morning began with a chuckle from heaven, a gleam in the eye of the Creator. God knew something no one else knew, and God was about to spring a surprise.

Meanwhile, on earth, human beings were feeling very comfortable with their religion. They had God neatly categorized, identified, and boxed. Rules helped; lots of them; and the wielding of power. Those in charge of God made sure they stayed in charge, with no dissent allowed. They were so sure of themselves that they even developed ways to eliminate any opposition. Just the other day, in fact, they took care of a Galilean rabble rouser who dared take them to task. They handed him over to the government, labeled him dangerous, and let the civilian authorities execute him. He was gone now, and God was right back where God belonged.

But they were wrong. God had the last laugh.

It happened on the third day. The first day was the time of the execution. The Romans took care of that with a gruesome crucifixion. That evening when the sun went down was the beginning of the Jewish Sabbath. For the next 24 hours, the second day, no one worked. God, however, was not resting but was preparing for the following morning, the third day. When the time was right, God made the next move and sprung the Great Surprise.

Some women were the first to hear God's laughter. It was a quiet chuckle in the morning air. At first, they didn't believe what they heard. It sounded something like, "He is risen!" But that couldn't be possible, could it? Then they saw for themselves! They saw for themselves and, when they recovered from their astonishment, joined in the fun.

One of the women said, "Let's go tell the others." So they did. But the men were in no mood for laughter. They had more serious things on their minds, like hiding and saving their necks. It was, after all, a dangerous time. It didn't take long, however, before even their hard hearts turned to chuckles. (Of course, they had to see for themselves first.) By now, God was laughing out loud. The men did hear – at least, most of them - and joined the women's Hallelujah Chorus.

They were all laughing because they now knew that the joke was on them, and on all the others who underestimated what God could do. They were all laughing because they now knew that, with God, even death is only a beginning and nothing in all creation is too impossible. They were all laughing, and their laughter reached the ears of friends, neighbors, outsiders, strangers, and to you, and to me.

God showed the world the difference between a midnight of sorrow and a dawn of joy. So it was that the tragedy ended with laughter. It was the laughter of eternity. Even you, even I, can join the fun.

Reflect:

What does the phrase "laughter of eternity" mean to you?

Where does God have the last laugh in your life?

Standing at the Door

(Acts 12:1-17)

You, Peter, stand knocking at the door in the middle of the night. The maid Rhoda opens the door, sees who it is, and is so excited that she closes the door on you again. You stand there waiting for someone to let you in.

You have come a long way in order to be here at this moment in time. Your journey began more than 10 years ago along the shores of the Sea of Galilee. Then you were a fisherman with a profitable business. You and your brother Andrew worked hard to make a living, and it paid off. You were married and lived in your family home.

Then Jesus entered your life, and everything changed. He asked you to follow him and learn from him. You were always impulsive, so you left your fishing nets behind. You and 11 others spent the better part of two years walking through both Jewish country and Gentile country. Your attitude and prejudices were challenged time after time. How could a Jew associate with a non-Jew? Why would anyone eat dinner with a tax collector? Why would a leper or a blind beggar be treated with respect?

You were always the one of the 12 who seemed best able to speak first and think later.. When Jesus told you to fish on the other side of the boat, you told him he didn't know what he was talking about.

151

When he decided to go to Jerusalem to celebrate the Passover, you argued that it was far too dangerous. When he asked the group what they thought of him, you were the one who said he was the Messiah. But when push came to shove on the night he was arrested, you were the one who swore three times that you didn't know him and had never met him. He died, and you went with the others into hiding.

On the third day, when the women came back from the grave with a ridiculous story about resurrection, you were the one to throw caution aside and run to see for yourself. Just 50 short days later, while you and other Jews celebrated Pentecost, you felt the power of God's Spirit moving among you and within you. Then you, the illiterate fisherman, stood in front of a crowd and told everyone what Jesus meant to you. You were so impressive that 3,000 people became followers.

Trouble seemed to follow you naturally. The authorities tried to shut you up, but you simply told them you could not keep quiet about what you had seen and heard. Recently, keeping the faith became even more dangerous. A new Herod is now in power, and he is as brutal as his grandfather Herod the Great. He beheaded your good friend James, who had been with you from the beginning. When Herod saw this execution made Jewish leaders happy, he arrested you yesterday morning and tossed you in jail. Knowing what happened to James, you were certain that your own death was just around the corner.

Herod wanted to make certain you stayed in jail. Acting on his orders, the soldiers took most of your clothes off and bound you with heavy chain. One guard stood on each side of you, with more guards at every exit. Your situation was desperate; it was also helpless.

Tonight, as you slept in the misery of your cell, you received a tap on the shoulder. In your half-sleep, you thought you were dreaming. Somehow, your chains fell off. You heard a voice telling you to get dressed. Was it a messenger from God? Then you were led past every one of the guards. The huge gate to the prison opened and you walked safely into the city streets. Then this strange apparition left you, and you were alone.

Now you stand at the door. The maid left, hopefully to tell someone you are here. You are still in danger. You know that with every bone in your body. You will have to go away after tonight; you know that as well.

Right now, however, you just want to get inside and tell your friends you are alive.

You knock again, and again. The door opens.

Reflect:

The early church experienced times of blessing
and also of immense pain.

They believed the hand of God supported them through
the highs and lows of their life.

Looking back, where have you seen the hand of God
giving you the support you needed?

In Jail

(Acts 16)

Yeah, I was there. Want to make something of it? You just want to know what happened? Okay, I'll tell you. It was like this.

I got picked up for shoplifting. They didn't ask no questions or nothing. They just tossed me in this stinking jail. All I see, all day and every day, are these stone walls. They don't feed us, and I have to hope my friends bring me something to eat now and then. There's no bathroom in here, and I'm chained to the wall anyway. You wonder why it stinks as bad as it does? Figure it out!

Last week two men got tossed in here with the rest of us. They were in rough shape. No clothes to speak of. Some self-righteous torturer had beaten them nearly to death with rods. The jailer chained them to the wall alongside the rest of us. He locked their feet in stocks so that their legs were spread apart. I'd seen it before. It was torture, pure and simple. So there they were, all day and into the night.

After they came to, I asked them what they did to get beaten up so bad. They told me their names were Paul and Silas. What they did was take some guy's business away from him. The way I understand it, they are followers of somebody called Jesus. They're also Jews, I guess. It's a little confusing to me.

What happened was, some guy had a slave girl who made him a lot of money by telling fortunes. That's a better racket than shoplifting, I'll tell you. This Paul saw what was happening, got mad, and said something like, "Evil spirit, leave!" After that, the slave girl couldn't tell fortunes any more. That made the owner mad.

One thing led to another, and here they were.

Come nighttime, they were pretty clear headed. They must have been hurting something awful, though. The strange thing is, they weren't moaning or complaining like I would have been. They were praying and singing hymns to their God. We were listening real careful. What else could we do? You can see how crowded it is in here.

While all this was happening, an earthquake hit us. We get a lot of earthquakes in this territory so we don't usually think too much about it. This was a bad one. The whole jail shook like crazy. I thought the rock walls were going fall down on us. It was so bad our chains came off and the jail doors busted open. I thought, man, we're free. But Paul begged us to stay. I don't know why we didn't run. There was just something about him.

Just then the jailer came running in. He was white as a ghost. You see, any escaped prisoner is on his head. He was ready to kill himself. Paul shouted to him. Told him we were all here. He brought in some torches to light up the place, and there we were.

I don't know what happened next, except for what I've been told. The jailer took Paul and Silas outside, and they were gone pretty much the rest of the night. Someone told me the jailer and his whole family made a complete turnaround and decided to be a Jesus follower like Paul was.

I guess I can understand that. There was something different about those two men. I've been thinking about them ever since. I keep wondering how they could pray and sing hymns after getting beaten up. And I still don't understand why we stayed in jail when we could have just walked out into the night. Maybe there's something there I don't know about. Maybe one day I'll find out.

Well, you wanted to know, so I told you. Now, will you do something for me? I haven't eaten for two days. Will you bring me some food?

Reflect:

What would you have done if you were a prisoner
in this Roman jail?

What do you think impressed the jailer so much
that he became a Jesus follower?

Who in your world best represents what it means
to be a Jesus follower? Why?

Dear Paul

(Philemon)

Sometime around 60 AD, Paul was in prison, probably in Rome. A slave named Onesimus[1] found his way to Paul. Onesimus had escaped from the household of Philemon,[2] who was a leader of the house churches in the valley where he lived. While Onesimus was with Paul, he became a follower of Jesus. He was a great help to Paul as well. Now, Onesimus was returning to his master. He carried with him a letter from Paul asking Philemon to reconcile with his former slave and to welcome him back. Philemon had several legal options open to him and, among them, could have rightfully executed the runaway. Paul was asking for a far different kind of justice. There is no record of how Philemon responded. What follows is an imaginary letter sent to Paul by Philemon's son Archippus.

Dear Paul:

Dad received your letter today when Onesimus returned home. He has been pacing around the house ever since. He has to make a hard choice, and I wouldn't want to be in his shoes. On the one hand, he has committed himself to following Jesus. He listened to your teachings and has followed them to the best of his ability. He helped you organize the churches in our valley and has been an important leader ever since. I know people respect him and look up to him. In fact, they look to his actions as an example of the way they need to live.

Paul, you were right when you said Dad loves the people in his congregation. He really does, and he shows it in a hundred ways. And, like you said, Jesus is important to him. It's not just lip service either. I can tell. He talks about Jesus and the things you taught him all the time.

But this thing with Onesimus has really thrown him for a loop. Everything he has ever known about slaves says that runaways must be punished. It's in the law, and it's the unwritten rule of our culture. He has every right to execute Onesimus or, at the very least, give him 39 lashes with the whip.

You want the impossible! You are asking Dad to live by a different rule of justice. You are asking him to treat the man like a brother and to welcome him home like the prodigal in Jesus' parable. You are asking him to put his faith on the line. You say this is the way of Christ.

I don't know what Dad is going to do. I don't know what I would do. I hear him now, walking around and talking to himself. Which way will he go? I guess we'll find out tomorrow.

Of course we will keep a room ready for you as you asked. You are always welcome in our home. Then you can see what has happened for yourself.

Following Jesus isn't very easy, is it?

Love,
A...

[1]Pronounced O-nes'-i-mus.
[2]Pronounced Phī-lē'-mon.

160

Reflect:

How does Paul's sense of justice compare with yours?

What would you have done if you were Philemon?

When have you faced a decision that placed your culture's sense of justice against the reconciliation themes of the Bible?
What did you do?

All Things New

(Revelation 21:5)

"See, I am making all things new."[1]

I don't think the Bible was ever intended to be a historical document. Nor do I think it is words on paper. Instead, I have always found it to be living, breathing, and forward-looking. Its stories find me wherever I am, speak to me of my current situation, and challenge me to find that place in life where grace, reconciliation, and justice come alive.

To put it another way, let me tell you one more story.

When I don't feel like being me, I sometimes become Abelard the clown.[2] *I put on white face, add a blue tear under my left eye, and paint on a lipstick smile. One Sunday not long ago, Abelard went to church.*

The worship service began with appropriate hymns and prayers and a sermon delivered by a woman pastor who brought a scripture story to life. Some time after she sat down, Abelard entered the room pulling a rope tied to a heavy bag. In plain sight of everyone in the room, he began to empty his bag. It was filled with rocks. Each rock was labeled. One said "guilt;" another "anger;" and still another "regret." A final rock was labeled "no good." Abelard clung tenaciously to his rocks, even

163

though they obviously weighed him down.

Soon, Sunny, another clown, came along. She saw Abelard and his rocks and tried to convince him to let them go. She told him she knew of a better way and that, if he would only let her, she could help ease his burden. Abelard refused, even turned away, and Sunny soon left.

Abelard tried to pick up his rocks and hold them close, as if they were the most precious thing in the world to him. They were so many and so heavy that they kept falling. He tried and tried and tried to cling to his precious stones. Finally, he dropped all his rocks, stood straight up, closed his eyes, and screamed.

Sunny came running back. This time, she carried a large cross that she placed in the center of a nearby table. Sunny spoke to Abelard about a new beginning and, this time, he listened. With her help he picked up the rocks, one at a time, and placed them around the cross. His last rock, his most precious rock, read "no good." Tenderly, he placed this final stone at the base of the cross. Then he stood straight one more time. This time, Abelard smiled.

[1]Revelation 21:5

[2]The real Abelard is a saint in the church's history. I like him because he always seemed to go against the grain and lived life on his own terms. He also fell in love with Eloise, which makes him pretty special in my book.

About the Author

Larry Beman is a United Methodist pastor/educator who sees himself more as a storyteller than a preacher. He likes to look in between the lines of the Bible stories to see what else might be there. He also has years of experience as a writer and editor. The result? A Chuckle from Heaven, with 42 stories and songs mined from the depths of scripture, biblical research, and his imagination

Larry lives in the western part of New York State with his wife, Barbara Bruce. He enjoys spending time in his carpenter shop, fishing a special Canadian lake, walking an Atlantic beach at sunrise, Sunday morning breakfasts at a coffee bar, and children's smiles.